Fundamentals for fashion retail STRATEGY PLANNING AND
IMPLEMENTATION

Charles Nesbitt

ISBN: 9781522816201

Also by Charles Nesbitt

FUNDAMENTALS FOR SUCCESSFUL AND SUSTAINABLE FASHION BUYING AND MERCHANDISING

FUNDAMENTALS FOR FASHION RETAIL ARITHMETIC, MERCHANDISE ASSORTMENT PLANNING AND TRADING

Table of Contents

PREFACE 5

INTRODUCTION 6

SCENARIO PLANNING 7

    The changing of the way we work 7

    Preparation of a Scenario Plan..9

    Selection of key drivers 10

    Brainstorming..11

    The eighty twenty rule 11

    Presentation of scenarios 12

STRATEGIC PLANNING 16

    Key performance indicators..22

STRATEGIC STAKEHOLDERS 24

    Business unit strategy 25

    Brand strategy 26

    Buying group strategy 28

    Customer strategy 36

    Product planning strategy..40

    Planning strategy...41

        Process 42

        Building the flow range plan 43

        Style and shape proportions 49

        Pricing structure...50

        Colour range...51

        Size architecture 52

        Allocations..53

    Trading...57

        Analysis options 59

    Sourcing strategy...60

        Supplier introduction 69

        Supplier manuals..70

        Style briefing 72

        Specification pack 73

        Supplier meetings 75

Negotiating...75

Technical strategy 77

Quality...79

Innovation 79

Social and environmental responsibilities 79

Safety 80

Fabric Technology...80

Fibres...81

Yarns...82

Selling strategy 82

Supplier strategy 86

Packaging strategy 92

Logistical strategy...96

Marketing strategy...106

Conclusion 107

INDEX...110

Referrals and acknowledgements 114

PREFACE

The process of buying and selling in some form or other of goods has been with us since time immemorial. Often when one stands in bewilderment in an elegant shopping mall and wonder how all the stores are able to effectively seduce the many shoppers trawling the wide corridors to readily part with their well-earned money while at the same time enabling them to possibly enjoy a wonderful social experience.

The plan of offering goods to the potential customer is a complicated one and is a science that involves many players whose individual contributions slot seamlessly together and are so perfectly co-ordinated that it provides the perception that it is the result of one individual concerted effort.

In order that this is most effectively done requires careful planning and formulation of a chain of events that are designed to deliver the envisioned objectives that will guarantee the development of a successful and sustainable business. An ideal saying is "if you do not know where you are going you may well end up somewhere else".

The reality is that we exist in a time that is complex, risky while also opportunistic but with more hostile competitors change happens more frequently with the result that it is becoming harder to manage businesses with increased workloads and challenges making it important to take quicker decisions.

It is therefore imperative that having a concise strategy in place helps to focus on the right customers and to link the philosophies and values to the customers and stakeholders in such a way that it is sustainable over the longer term. The strategy informs, focuses attention and inspires performance. It should be simple, clear and compelling while still being multifaceted and challenging. Consistency is absolutely vital to provide the road map to be followed by the operational and tactical planned activities. If these principles are not strictly adhered to in all likelihood the unsuccessful execution of the strategy can be the unpleasant consequence.

In order to avoid this happening there needs to be a pre-planned setting of goals that are realistic, specific and quantifiable that are achieved via a set design of tactical operational actions. Strategy can be described as a basic process that leads change in the business. To do this a view of the future is required in order to know what needs to be done to operate in the new world. The end result should be the addition of sustainable value to the customer which will ensure the survival and future success of the organisation.

Leading companies are well aware that to maintain the competitive edge and achieve success they need to have an effective strategic plan in place.

This book endeavours to try and outline the rudimentary key principles and mechanisms by which this happens and should be helpful to students, people in retailing and those who are maybe considering a career in the industry. For those who already are part of the fashion buying and merchandising community this book will be beneficial in that it provides a complete simplified overview of all the integral activities and roles that go to make up the topic and thereby will provide a broader insight into their own career.

The material of the book, other than that specifically referenced is the result of the author's own exposure to the subject during a career spanning thirty five years at a major retail organisation in Southern Africa, the support from colleagues, mentors, interaction with suppliers and own research. There has been some cross referencing to other books or technical material but the book focuses largely at a higher level on the key principles, concepts and theories and hence there is none or very little mention of retailers by name or technological packages for some key activities such as planning, allocating, critical path management, logistics and the like.

INTRODUCTION

It is always difficult to accomplish anything without a plan. Whether it is a sporting event, a dinner, preparing a lecture or managing a business, a strategic plan is required. The strategic plan enables business leaders to prioritise where to spend time, human resources and financial capital in order to deliver the best outcomes.

The action is implemented through the use of specific and measurable objectives together with tactics to ensure that the clearly stated mission as to why the company exists is achieved. A point to note is that the more adventurous the strategy, the higher is the risk involved but may still reap more reward. It is important therefore to reiterate that the mission must be realistic and adaptable.

While it is acknowledged the strategic plans are required to be flexible in order to maintain the best possible competitive advantage and adapt to achieve their set down objectives there are unchanging values of the company that exist to serve as a point of reference to provide guidance in the process of strategic decision making. These primary ideals form the vision of the company and are expressed in the mission statement which communicates the ideology of the company remaining relatively constant. In short it is the reason for the existence of the firm and outlines the visionary goals which will be pursued in order that the mission will be achieved. The strategic plan answers the question as to why which differs from the business or operational plan which answers the question how. The objectives and tactics required in order to achieve the strategic plan will be reflected in an operational plan. It must be noted that even if the core business activities change completely, the ideologies of the company will remain unchanged. Examples of core values are integrity, innovation, good customer service and social responsibility.

The purpose or reason for the existence of the company is also likely to remain unchanged, for example, a main reason for existence of a company is most likely to make a profit but what is important is the definition of how the profit will be generated and should portray the firm as it really is.

The visionary goals of the company which are selected by management are normally at a relatively high level and are probably in the long term that the company will continually strive for. Such goals can be quantitative but may also be more general. An example could be to strive to be seen as the foremost leader in its field.

A standstill assessment of the current status will identify what needs to change and that which is not performing. The purpose will be to establish where the focus should be applied and question if the current incumbents being held responsible are the most suitable and whether or not additional resources are required.

A strategic plan is required to cater for the consistently changing and more complex environments which need to be identified through detailed strengths, weaknesses, opportunities and threats analysis of both internal and external factors. Examples of these may be a stable internal infrastructure, exchange rate fluctuations, and new competitor activity, potential new markets and the like. The plan should provide a view of the future so it is clear as to what the business is required to do in order to survive in the new world and best serve the customer in a consistent manner.

While it is great to have a strategic plan, it is equally important that the plan is regularly reviewed and updated and is followed relentlessly. For this to happen effectively the format has to be efficient, flexible and interactive. As planning is an ongoing process, so the setup must allow for information to be captured, shared and updated in real time which will alert the retailer to the warning signs as to what could happen in particular situations and have alternative ideas readily in place that can be easily and quickly implemented.

SCENARIO PLANNING

From a broader perspective it is wise to evaluate the forecasts of your own and respected scenario planners to attempt to understand any possible impacts on the business and trading environment that may or may not evolve in the future. Scenario analysis is used to formulate a picture of the potential trading landscape in the longer term. Previously strategic planning was almost simply the financial extrapolation of past history going forward with hardly any qualitative discussion about the social conditions where the combined effect of various factors can have a significant impact. Some of these that we think we know about are forward trends, demographic shifts and the impact of new technologies. Those which we have no knowledge of are the uncertainties which are almost unpredictable such as currency rates, interest rates, outcomes of elections, impact of dominant political leaders, effect of political sanctions and the road ahead in terms of high risk hotspots such as the circumstances currently being experienced in the middle east, the consequence of an overwhelming influx of refugees into various countries, fads and fashions and technological innovations.

The changing of the way we work

The way we work in the longer term is highly likely to dramatically change. There is no dispute that the manner in which tasks are completed is rapidly adapting to suit a totally new environment. The advancement of technology, connectivity and the expectations of both employers and employees are demanding that the economic activities be radically reviewed.

There is an ever increasing trend to relocate resources from the traditional high density centres such as Hong Kong, Tokyo, London, Paris and the like because of high living costs, fast increasing rentals, and salaries which are being outpaced by costs. As a result the purchasing power of residents is being severely diminished and therefore this tendency is forcing organisations to relocate to areas where it is cheaper to live and conduct business. Technology has aided this process as it is easier to operate from remoter areas and still have access through tools such as Google, Dropbox, Skype and the like which makes it just as easy to service customers as effectively no matter where the base location is. The base link ups could also be temporary in that desks could be rented with all the required technological facilities, boardroom or conference facilities supported by the appropriate equipment and catering requirements thus saving investment in permanent structures.

Apart from being able to conveniently work from different sites the necessity for a substantial portion of the workforce no longer have to negotiate the traffic or use public transport daily and therefore the surplus time saving can be productively utilised. There are instances that those firms who find it difficult to adapt to this newer culture and stubbornly maintain a level of mistrust have experienced a depletion of suitable staff and productivity as the workforce prefer to pursue a flexible option. It is important that the mind shift of acknowledging that the quality delivery of tasks should be the measure of productivity and not the actual time spent in the office.

The trend has evolved that an incumbent is no longer a specialist in one field all their life. With the ongoing development of new processes, technologies and systems in order to be successful there is a continual need for education and re-education. One big degree for a lifelong job at one corporation is being replaced by a culture of a repeatable cycle of learning then work, then learn again and work to sustain competitiveness in the labour market. It is fact that where in the past job hopping carried a considerable stigma, this is now more than ever becoming the norm.

In days gone by, the evidence of consistent job hopping on an applicant's resume hinted that in all likelihood presented a negative perception that the candidate probably had a people issue and did not get on with others, could not hold down a job, was disloyal and could not commit to a long term relationship.

The reality is that the opposite is becoming the actuality especially with regard to advancing through a continual learning and relearning process and the new job hopping millennia's are now perceived to possess a higher learning curve, perform better and deliver above expectations as they pursue the drive to make a favourable impression and assert themselves in a shorter time period with each employer.

Because such employees are continually challenging themselves outside their comfort zones they are typically over achievers who deliver a significant contribution to the bottom line which stands them in good stead before they move on to new opportunities every two to four years. It is believed that the learning curve tends to flatten after three years so in fact regular job hopping has become crucial to ensure a stable career growth.

It nevertheless can remain a concern for companies as there is a continual requirement to invest in new staff but the upside is that the rapid growth of the organisation and the worry of the loss of intellectual property to competitors is less threatening because the swift change makes the impact of the loss of such intellectual assets soon to be outdated.

The world is also seeing an exponential growth of entrepreneurs who with their specialised knowledge, offer their services on a short term basis simply by working as freelancers or contractors. With a wide-ranging exposure they enhance their skills and are thereby able to raise their rates or acquire additional freelancers to assist them and consequently grow their personal wealth.

Preparation of a Scenario Plan

Scenario planning can be defined as the blending of the known and unknown into a consistent future point of view. All our knowledge that we have is about the past, most of which can be described as we don't know what we don't know, a smaller percentage is knowing what it is that we don't know, and the smallest percentage is being aware of what it is that we actually do know. The conclusion is therefore the knowledge that is required in order to make good decisions is mostly beyond our comprehension.

Coupled to the knowledge base, the different types of futures can be categorised into "possible" or that which might happen based on future knowledge, that which is "plausible" which is what could happen and therefore depends on current knowledge, that what is "probable" based on current trends and lastly that which is "preferable" which is what we want to happen based on value judgments.

The proportionate levels of knowledge inputted into the different types of future

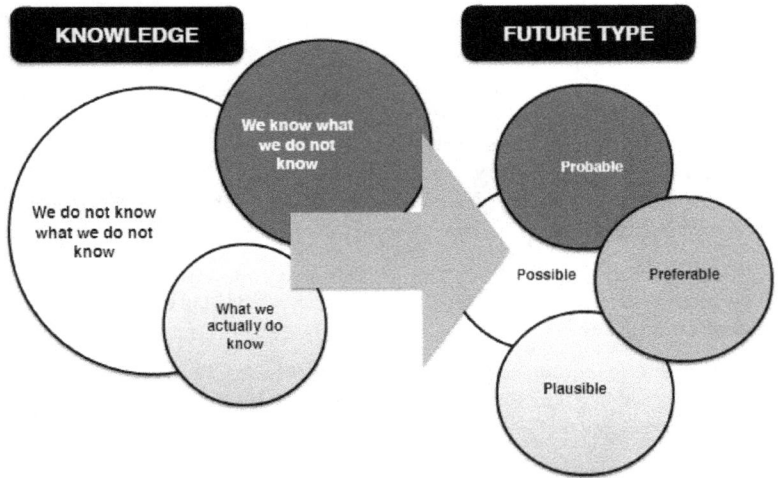

Scenarios can be described as possible views of the world in a narrative or story form which enables better informed forward decisions being able to be made which is likely to assist in the formulation of a successful strategy. It should be noted that scenarios do not predict the future but rather highlight those drivers that are most likely to influence the future and form part of the strategic management toolbox which consists of traditional methods which focus on the past while scenario planning tools focus on the future. By combining both the past and future the strategic thinking process is therefore stronger and enables better responsiveness, improved flexibility as well as generates a competitive advantage.

The creation of such scenarios follow a simple structured sequence of events where conscious long term judgments such as the identification of the major influences and factors within varying situations can bring about significant changes to the way business is done and deliver a diversity of results. Scenarios can be created through the grouping of complimentary influences into a framework of a number of "what if" situations. The number of these may then be reduced to an amount through amalgamation or elimination to end up with a manageable quantity of scenarios which would possibly have the greatest effect should they occur.

Selection of key drivers

After both an internal and external environmental scan is done, the consequence is the identification the key factors or subjects which may well decide the future nature of the environment in which the organisation will be operating. These forces will form the pillars of the areas which need to be examined and the specific definition of those drivers that will form the base of the different scenarios. Once the important topics are acknowledged, they are used to create scenarios which deliver alternative outcomes and should include the important predictable as well as the unknown outcomes. Typical examples of such drivers are those that represent the social, economic, technological, environmental, globalisation and political aspects.

The environmental scan will include an internal analysis of the company in terms of the strengths and weaknesses as well as an external scrutiny of the threats and opportunities which may or may not exist. Part of the scan will include an exploration of the industry that the business operates within. This will include the examination of the barriers that exist to enter the industry, the existing supplier infra-structure, customer base and evidence of substitution products as well as the rivalry intensity that is present amongst the participants.

After assessing the environmental scan, the firm will match those strengths they possess to their benefit and address the weaknesses as well as acknowledge the threats to the possible opportunities that may exist.

The macroeconomic environment factors also need to be taken into consideration, sometimes referred to as the PEST analysis (which is the acronym for political, economic, social and technological) that will impact on the firms operations.

Political factors include government regulations and legal issues under which the company must operate such as tax policy, employment laws and regulations, environment boundaries that may exist, trade restrictions and tariff structures as well as the overall political stability.

Economic facets that will influence the scenario planning process will be the economic growth, interest rates, inflation and exchange rates.

Social factors such as demographic and cultural aspects in the macroeconomic environment which will affect the customer needs and market penetration are typically health consciousness, population growth, the spread of age distribution and attitude to careers.

Technological factors such as automation, research and development will have significant impacts on production efficiencies and the extent that tasks need to be outsourced.

Brainstorming

Before we proceed any further it is valuable to describe a simple brainstorming process.

There are many techniques of brainstorming, some of which are more sophisticated than others. A very popular, basic and easy to use methodology, although it may be slower than other processes, is through the use of common sticky notelets.

All that is required is an isolated room with a clear wall and maybe a flip chart to list comments and park some issues for later discussion. The number of participants should not be too few but also not too large. In most cases the ideal quantity should be no more than fifteen which is a controllable amount that normally can be comfortably managed by the facilitator.

Prior to the commencement of the session the key drivers or pillars which were identified in the environmental analysis stage must be prominently indicated as the headings under which the sticky notelets will be randomly stuck on the wall which have the advantage that they can be removed or relocated as discussion progresses.

As is the case with the majority of brainstorming sessions, the generation of ideas invariably stimulate the creation of others which are pasted on the wall and the participants can move the posts around the wall under the designated headings as they wish. The process is relatively user friendly and therefore it is also easy for newcomers to grasp the concept and enjoy participating.

The illustrated example below assumes that the key drivers that will serve as the headings on the clear wall have been defined as political, social, technological, economic and environment.

The participants are then able to actively write their ideas on the notelets and paste them under the relevant heading.

Once all the ideas are exhausted and are evident on the wall under the appropriate headings the next stage will be to identify those that are important versus those that are not in terms of their levels of impact and uncertainty on the future. In order that this is done effectively the application of the eighty twenty rule is critical so that only those factors which are most relevant are focused on. Just allowing a number of topics to be randomly selected in terms of their perceived importance often results in those topics which are purely of interest being selected as opposed to those that are prioritised according to the commercial significance.

The eighty twenty rule

The eighty twenty rule, also known as the Pareto principle, recognises that a principle of eighty percent of the result is delivered by twenty percent of the effort or participants.

Prime examples in retailing is, for example, in the context of stores it is probable that twenty percent of the stores deliver eighty percent of the sales and deserve the proportionate dedication of energy and focus, as does the thick middle sizes such as medium and large and therefore should always be in stock. Core base colours such as white, black, naturals and greys also contribute largely to the sales and should always be evident in volume. It is clear that certain styling features will likewise guarantee the bulk of sales and should be finalised first and certain peak trading periods such as holidays or special events will contribute largely to the total seasonal sales and must be managed very carefully in terms of production planning and delivery scheduling.

Once the important topics are identified, the use of them to create scenarios which deliver alternative outcomes should include the important predictable inferences as well as fictional conclusions.

The next step is to integrate these key influences and thereby create a framework or scenario matrix. The linking of some of the influences can take place where the characteristic of one factor may be relevant to another while, on the other hand this may not always be the case. The brainstorm participants therefore arrange the elements into groups that have relevance and make some sense. The amount of groups that emerge will be dependent on the number of elements available to contemplate. While this process is in progress it is possible that new groupings may be added while others could be removed. As these clusters of elements materialise, the creation of the mini scenarios may be linked together based on their similarities or mutual influence and eventually a process of rationalising and absorption can take place to condense the mini scenarios into two or three core scenarios. All of the above will entail extensive debate before common ground is met in order to agree the fundamental insights into what the really imperative issues are applicable to the organisation. Once this stage is achieved, because of the intimate understanding of the participants that has developed, it will be almost instinctive without any reference to any formal report to know how to cope with potential issues should and when they materialise.

Presentation of scenarios
The final two or three scenarios that are constructed need to be written up in a formal format to serve as a consistent guideline for team leaders to base their strategy on. The report will in essence be more qualitative rather than be peppered with intense detail although reference may be made to tabular work and diagrams but in whatever emphasis this happens, the report needs to remain factual.

An example of the simplistic building of a scenario plan using the process described above is depicted below

Key headings and notelets pasted below on the clear wall with the annotation of importance of each comment in terms of impact relative to uncertainty is depicted as follows

POLITICAL	SOCIAL	TECHNOLOGICAL	ECONOMIC	ENVIRONMENT
Influence of global governments	Increasing population	Increasing reliance on technology	Declining trade of traditional commodities	Increasing acceptance of environment awareness
1 Li/Hu	2 Mi/Mu	3 Hi/Lu	4 Li/Mu	5 Mi/Mu
Influence of dominant world leaders	Aged more economically active	Improved health environment through better technologies	Globalisation	Continued degradation of natural environment
6 Mi/Mu	7 Hi/Lu	8 Mi/Mu	9 Mi/Lu	10 Hi/Lu
Global conflict	Cultural transformation through globalization, immigration and technology	Newer and cleaner renewable energy resources now viable	New technologies creating channels for empoyment	Declining water quality
11 Hi/Mu	12 Li/Mu	13 Hi/Hu	14 Li/Hu	15 Hi/Mu
Terrorism	Increased life expectancy and quality health support	Increasing technological devices making shopping easier	Evolution of single global currency	Declining air quality and increased energy consumption
16 Hi/Hu	17 Mi/Lu	18 Li/Hu	19 Mi/Hu	20 Mi/Hu
Influence of key election results	Rural areas being developed increased urbanisation	Combination of technologies to make on line trading become economically efficient	Traditional employment approach creating unemployment	Impact of global climate change
21 Li/Lu	22 Li/Lu	23 Mi/Lu	24 Li/Lu	25 Li/Mu
Influence of non government organisations				
26 Li/Hu				

Uncertainty

Low (Lu) – very that activity will happen in the way that we expect

High (Hu) – no certainty as to what will happen

Med (Mu) – somewhere in between

Impact

Low (Li) – effect of activity will deliver low results

High (Hi) – effect of activity will deliver high results

Med (Mi) – somewhere in between

A Scattergram below illustrates according to the corresponding shapes the relative significance of impact and uncertainty of each comment

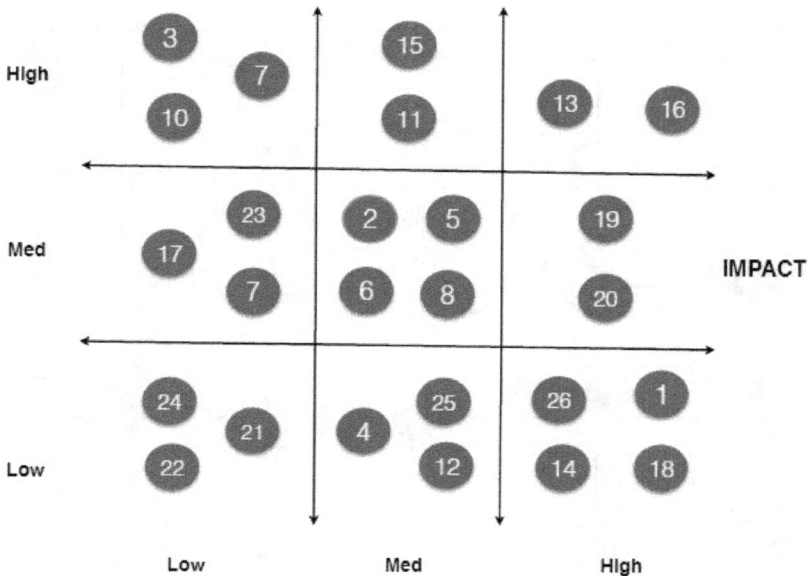

UNCERTAINTY

The two highest uncertainty and highest impact critical external factors (right top of the matrix) which will be selected according to our model will be

- Terrorism
- New and cleaner renewable energy resources which are now economically viable

The three most critical internal factors in terms of impact and uncertainty which will be selected are

- Increase in market penetration through innovative and technological methodologies
- Availability of safe retail space
- Supplier management and sustainability

In the scenario workshop the participants will need to consider the world of the future taking into account the external and internal factors and the influence they will have in creating the environment in which trade will take place.

During the process of imagining the world of the future it is essential that participants are not influenced by personal opinions such as not believing it possible, mistrust and relying on intuition but should rather focus on the plausibility perspective. By way of illustration the drafting of the scenario of the future period must be therefore be done taking into account the following types of points

- What will the world be like going forward? To do this take into account the events that brought change to where you are now and project those events that will influence the world going forward.
- In building a picture of a future world consideration should be given to the effect of current indicators are not necessarily a foregone conclusion should they change significantly. As an example, if the borrowing interests increase, the growth of the economy will probably be undermined and consequently the currency in relation to other currencies will be worth less. However even if the interest rates are conversely reduced unless the domestic demand for product is strong enough, the currency could still deteriorate. The possibility of exporting more product, or attracting more tourism will have a positive influence on growth as will attracting foreign investors. Commodity prices will also change the landscape dramatically such as a weak oil price will enable cheaper costs but it may not be weak but is gaining strength so in this case will have the reverse effect.
- Will your organisation exist in this new world going forward? What would you look like? Are you going to be global? Will you be virtual or physical? What will your customer look like? What will your organisational structure look like?
- The drafting and presentation of the scenario does not have to be off the wall but above all should be creative.

The main uses of scenarios is to provide a common language for ongoing forward discussions, assess the risks involved when taking specific decisions, assist in the evaluation of current strategies as well as in the development of new strategies.

Scenarios provide clues as to what the strategic drivers of the future might be, how they may interact and in what way they may affect the organisation. The identification of robust strategies that will be able to survive future scenarios is key and are able to assist in detecting early warning indicators to know what to do in the occurrence of such events, some of which may be catastrophic beyond control, wide in scope and rapidly moving. Examples of such events could be a stock market collapse, a terrorist attack or disrupted water and electricity supply.

One certain conclusion about change is that change will happen. The skill is, through scenario planning is to identify in what way organisations will change. Examples of how they are likely to change could be such as from an autocratic environment to an empowerment one, from a structured life to an unstructured life, from a volume based production base to a need for speed to market base, from high predictability based on historical trends to a world of uncertainty, from slow change to rapid change and ambiguity, from reliance on processes to reliance on people, from structured hierarchical organisations to alliances and coalitions, from avoiding risk to managing risk.

The final message to take note of is that the traditional strategic planning processes are no longer sufficient on their own but need the support of well thought out perceptions of the future.

STRATEGIC PLANNING

The commencement of the process to draft and implement a strategic plan follows a set sequence of events that form the foundation of a blueprint that needs to be followed to develop a sustainable plan of action going forward.

The type of points that need to be addressed in the drafting of a plan is to know what the vision together with the corresponding mission is. The relevant customer and their desires specific to the retailer have to be intimately clear.

The strategy ought to be aimed specifically at them in order that the purpose and values of the business is linked by the strategy to the right customer and the other stakeholders. It is therefore important that the strategy is sustainable over the longer term through clear communication, that it directs the focus and effort and thereby energises and inspires people to consistently perform at optimal levels.

Competitors should be clearly identified as well as the factors that will influence both the customer and the competitors of the future. Added to this the competitors are becoming increasingly hostile in a global market which adds complexity bringing with it more challenges requiring additional thought to transform ideas into action in a much shorter space of time often with limited resources. It is therefore absolutely imperative that the retailer should know as much about their competitors as possible and should in fact construct a dossier on each of their foremost challengers. Knowing who the direct and indirect contenders are and how they are performing in the market place, what can be learnt from their operations, what their strengths and weaknesses are, how different they are, the frequency and what media is used to advertise as well as what pricing strategy is employed will assist in the intimate understanding of competitors.

There are two basic types of competitive advantage which are the cost factor whereby the product is the same or similar in form and function to competitors but is made available at a lower price. The second advantage is the difference in the form of added value the product possesses compared to other products on offer in the market. The strategic activities may include plans to create the competitive advantage in one way or the other through the processes as outlined below.

In the strategic planning process the weaknesses need to be emphasised in order to minimise risks, the strengths must to be continuously capitilised upon while at the same time the appreciation of any threats to the business which may hamper the progress has to be taken into account. With all these factors in mind the plan of appropriate operational activities must be formulated in such a way that they are aligned to the vision of the company and support the basis of the strategy.

A firm's strengths are its resources and capabilities to gain competitive advantage and typical of these are patents, reputable brands, reputation, cost advantages and access to effective distribution networks.

The absence of certain strengths can be interpreted as weaknesses and could include factors such as absence of patent protection, weak brands and lack of reputation, high cost structures and poor distribution channels.

The external environmental analysis may result in the identification of the emergence of opportunities for growth and profit as well as certain threats. Examples of opportunities could be the evolvement of new customer needs, development of new technologies, the relaxation of regulations and the possible removal of international trade barriers. The opposite of the opportunities could in turn be seen as the threats to the firm such as the shift away from the products by the customers, the emergence of substitute products, new regulations and the imposition of international trade barriers.

This dependable interpretation of the strategy will enable the planning of management activity that is used to set the priorities, focus energy and resources, strengthen the operational events while ensuring all the key stakeholders are aligned in such a way that the overall company strategic goals are achieved. A documented strategic plan is formulated which communicates the goals and the operational activities that are required to achieve them. Management of the plan must ensure that the processes are systematically coordinated and the resources and actions are aligned with the mission, vision and strategy throughout the organisation.

The framework and methodologies of managing the strategic plan broadly follow the same sequence of phases which are that the understanding of the external and internal environments is developed, the formulation of the strategy is documented, a corresponding operational plan of activities required to achieve the strategic goals is drafted and lastly, the evaluation and sustainability of the plan is managed and continually refined through performance measurement, communications and data reporting.

Diagrammatically the process cycle of strategic planning can be depicted as follows

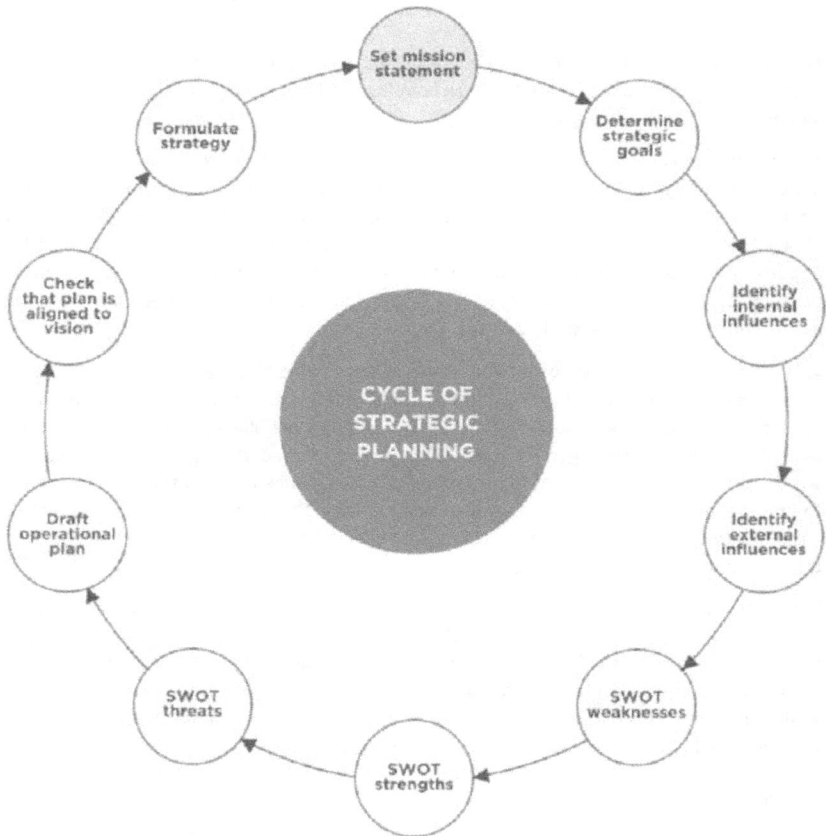

By way of illustration a hypothetical retailer has been formed which follows the creation of the strategy and the subsequent operational plan. In broad terms the business firstly documents its vision which describes the blue sky dream of becoming a preferred retailer which offers clothing that represents exceptional value, is up to date with current trends and is purposeful in both form and function.

The company has a mission to expertly fulfill the customers' needs transparently in such a way that they can be trusted and sustain a high level of integrity.

In order that this can be achieved adequately the set of goals need to be identified that are realistic, are able to be benchmarked and measured. In the simplistic model outlined below there are basically three goals that need to be focused on which are growing market penetration by one percent through the optimum use of media, expand real estate to cater for all regions and develop and implement tools of measurement of supplier performance to ensure the optimum delivery of product to maximise profit opportunities.

In order to remain focused it is imperative to identify where the strong points are such as a loyal customer base and trustworthy and reliable suppliers and to constantly focus on protecting these qualities. On the other hand it should be acknowledged that they may well be behind the rest of the field in terms of technologically advanced competitors who are reaping the benefits of digital retail channels and should grasp the potential development of such vehicles as a wonderful opportunity to acquire similar benefits that the competitors do.

A simplistic example of a strategic plan of a hypothetical retailer can be as outlined below

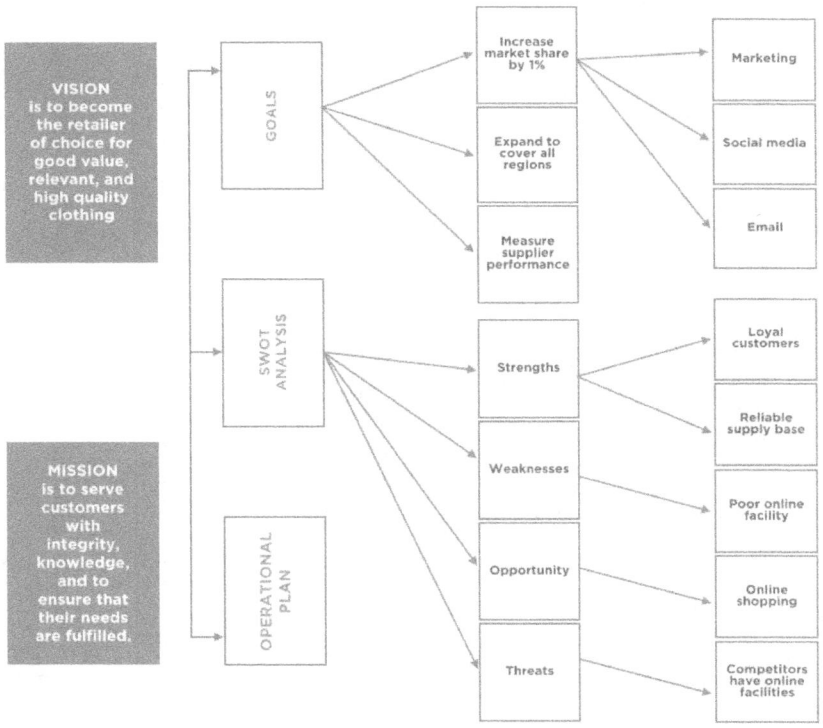

As has been stated, the strategic thinking delivers what is desired to be delivered while the operational aspect provides guidance as to how the objectives are going to materialise. The example of the hypothetical retailer who wishes to be a retailer of choice may wish to use the advantage derived from loyalty programmes which could be in the form of discount coupons, the publication of own brand magazines and derive the benefit of sophisticated analysis of the consumer data base to gain better understanding of their customer profile.

The desired sales outlet expansion will have to be achieved through opening of new stores, the remodeling and enlargement of existing stores, expansion of newer formats with the exploitation of those categories which offer the most potential opportunities and the development of an on line sales channel all of which will demand additional location sites, design and IT resources.

The effective measurement of supplier efficiencies will require measurement tools and a reporting infrastructure which will preferably be available on line and provide for a system of penalties for underperformers and incentives for those suppliers who exceed expectation

The corresponding operational plan for the strategic plan above will therefore possibly look like

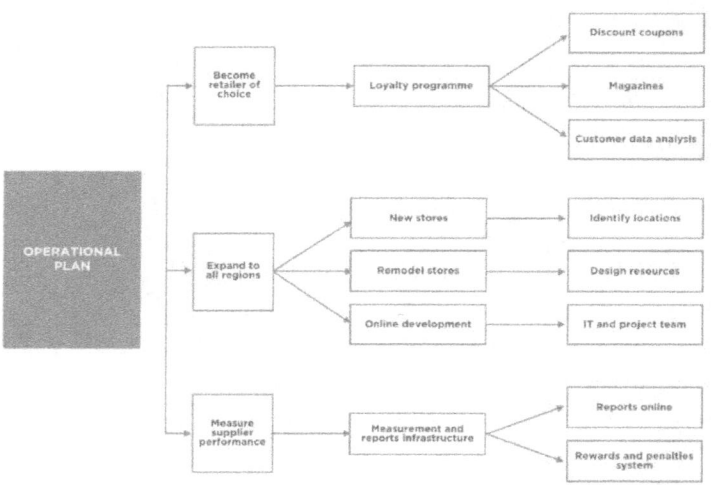

The consequences of poorly thought out strategies can be devastating. There are many examples of once extremely successful chains whose buildings that were landmarks are today parking garages. Retailers who have a tendency to doubt outlooks are often displayed through the rear view mirror images which tells us from where we have come has always worked and the subsequent question asked is more often than not "if it is not broken why change?"

The very successful, intelligent captains of such firms often succumb to the destruction of once successful business for a number of reasons. The fear of change is more often than not the cause because the potential is not viewed as an opportunity but rather seen as a risk. When there is a trend being followed by competitors or new entries to the market an air of arrogance takes hold and the dogged belief is upheld that the current trading philosophies which are set in concrete will withstand the onslaught and any other unfamiliar options are doomed to failure.

Taking the importance of new strategic objectives seriously is seen at times as just another routine task on the calendar which needs to be completed but in reality the focus quickly apathetically returns to complete the current responsibilities as before to sustain the operation.

The lack of the leaders who see the big picture and miss out on the benefits in total can be extremely damaging. In their place is only those who resolutely continue the practice of working within their own relevant areas of control and comfort zones and do not consequently contribute to the achievement of an overall vision. Invariably it is the personal objective that dominates which is one of self-preservation as is reflected in the view that as long as their area has performed within the required parameters any failures that may arise cannot be attributed to them.

Similarly some organisations, characteristically those that are family driven or are by nature very staid with autocratic leadership frequently lack imagination to foresee change or are reluctant to "think out of the box" and consequently there is an unwillingness to innovate. When such an approach is challenged it is often met with obstinacy to hold on to what's more certain, defined and secure which is in the present. The effect is that the argument for change is often justified by making the situation sound less critical than it really is and is stereotypically confirmed by erroneous comparisons to other existing case studies.

The success of retailers is frequently measured by the scale of operations and share value rather than by the product quality, shopping experience and resultantly the usage of the phrase "customer service" becomes trite and is nothing but just a throw away statement.

In many circumstances operations were in recent years dominated by the availability of easy credit at stores where the needs of the customer were broadly projected and the product was bought in high volumes across a limited number of categories to lever better prices from vendors. The driving force was to sell them as quickly as possible using mediocre service. Consequently innovation and revitalised selling formats were almost totally stagnant for many years.

The reality is that the consumer has become conscious to this fact and it does not inspire them any longer to remain loyal to a specific brand but rather to source out the retailers who are sincere in their messages, offer service of difference whereby the customers can truly appreciate a better experience. Much of the success of the newer revolutionary retailers is that they have identities that the consumer associate with which may be cultural such as an eastern philosophies, sporting associations with an emphasis on lifestyle and role models where the markets are not dependent on mass and discount but on meaning and have become communities in themselves.

The point needs to be made that it takes some bold mind shifts when the writing is on the wall that failure is imminent and the need to manage the way out of the situation calls for outside interventions, new strategies and tactics and respect in order to emerge on the other side of the storm successfully.

Key performance indicators

There have been many portrayals of key performance indicators over time such as "what is measured gets done", "if you do not measure results you are unable to distinguish between success and failure", and "if you are not able to measure it you cannot manage or improve it". In summary it is the true identification of strategic measurements of inputs, project and operational processes which results in the degree of successful or unsuccessful deliverables.

For stakeholders to be able to check whether the performance is on track to achieve the strategic objectives it is measured against a suite of pre-set performance indicators. The most common performance pointers which are assigned targets that will deliver the desired financial requirements, are the following.

    Sales
    Markdowns
    Buying margin
    Sales margin
    Stock forward cover
    Stock annual turn
    Return on inventory investment

It is absolutely imperative that these indicators are clearly understood by all members of the retail team both in the head office and stores and what the role is that they individually play in the support of them.The measures are almost always referred to in financial reports as share holders utilise these to determine their level of confidence in the company performance.

The market share measurement is a key performance indicator which is a simple calculation of the company's proportion of the total market. It is essential to consider it in detail as part of the strategy planning process as sales figures independently do not necessarily reflect how well the company is performing relative to its competitors.

The value of the total market is not always readily available and often the involvement of market research companies which have as many retail companies subscribed as they can recruit and through accumulation of each subscribers sales defined in various categories and total are able to determine relatively accurately each subscribers share and communicate the individual retailers results in detail, usually on a quarterly basis, without divulging other member's information.

Although market share reflects the strength of the company in the market it does not necessarily reflect the profitability. The advantage of a high market penetration is that it improves the buying power and higher volumes enable the benefit of economies of scale and thereby the retailer is able to negotiate keener cost prices.

The key drivers of improving market share is that of quality in terms of form and function of the product, the price competitiveness, the effectiveness of marketing campaigns and the network of stores that expose the products to the customer.

In a number of cases it may be preferred to actually decrease market share of product such as where there may be a low margin strategy and therefore the more that is sold the higher is the pressure on the overall profitability and a price war may be provoked.

However it is not only the monetary results that are the key deliverables. There are also the qualitative perceptions of the strategic intent that indicate the the degree of of success of a plan.

Other qualitative performance indicators may exist such as a reduction of the customer waiting time factor where the actual can be measured to a set target which will translate into improved customer retention.

Internal strategic objectives could be the introduction of enhanced systems or processes which will improve efficiency, effectiveness and time savings against set targets.

Organisational capacity improvement might be achieved through intensified training, resources investment and operational processes design which can be expected to deliver efficiency and logistical time saving.

Brand awareness can be improved through technological system enhancements with strategic marketing techniques.

Social awareness and programmes may be established with specific targets being set in terms of goodwill perception and is compared to actuals derived through various means such as data collection from loyalty programmes, questionnaires, membership enrolment and social media analysis.

Good KPI's provide an objective way to see if a strategy is working, offer a comparison to guage the degree of performance change over time, focus employees attention as to what matters that are most probable to succeed, they provide a common language for communication of results that are valid to ensure the measurement of the right things and are certifiable with reference to accurate data integrity.

The balanced scorecard

KPI's are the progress indicators in terms of achieving a successful outcome through the monitoring of the implementation and effectiveness of an organisation's strategy.

The creation of a balanced scorecard may be done through the establishment of target values for each identified KPI and an actual score based on historical values and trends. A certain amount subjectivity is established through applying some weighting to the strategical intent. This activity provides a framework that not only provides performance measurements but also identifies what should be done and be measured which truly enables the execution of a strategy.

Apart from ensuring that the financial funds are in place as a priority to allow for the efficient operation of the company through resourceful and accurate provision of data, the balanced scorecard recommends the analysis of the organisation from other perspectives as well. These include the learning and growth perspective which comprises of employee training and corporate cultural attitude related to both individual and corporate self improvement. In the current rapid technological change it is becoming increasingly necessary for knowledge to be acquired through a continual learning process. It is therefore essential for metrics to be put in place to ensure that sufficient funds are in place in order to accommodate this.

The third business process perspective is to have metrics in place in order to assess whether or not the the business is running well enough to have the products and services that sufficiently conform to the customer requirements. The design of these measurements need to be determined by the right people who intimately understand the mission of the company.

Lastly, the customer perspective has been developed by a retail management philosophy that stresses the importance of customer focus and service. Poor performance from this perspective can only lead to the decline of trading performance even though current sales performance may not immediately indicate this.

STRATEGIC STAKEHOLDERS

In a clothing retail environment the typical individual stakeholder areas need to focus on their independent strategies for a specific period of time that together must be aligned to meet the overall company strategy. It is therefore imperative that the different areas are scrutinized and activities are adapted to ensure that this objective is achieved.

Illustratively the various pertinent strategic focus areas are depicted as follows

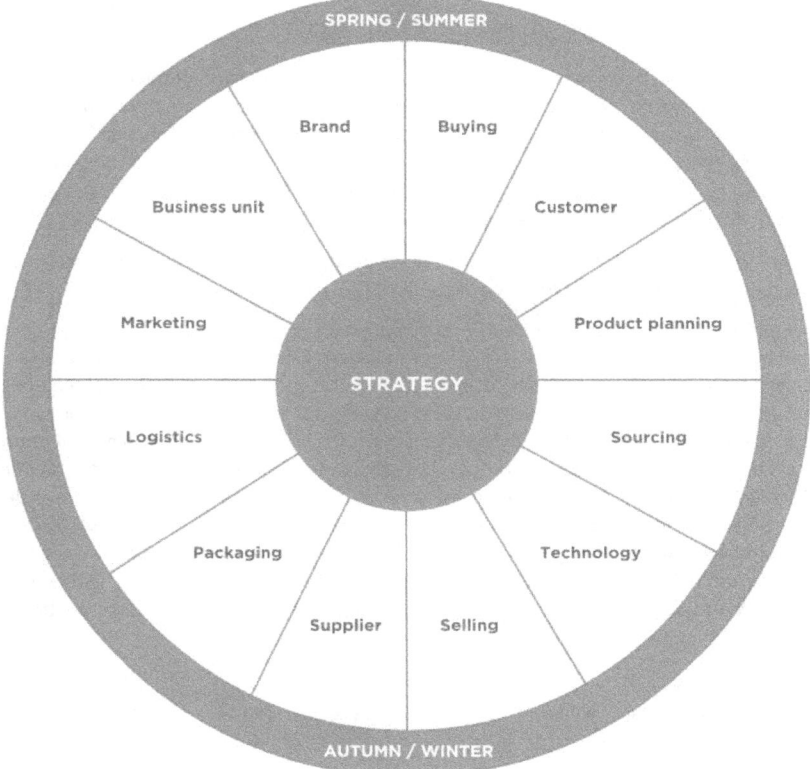

Business unit strategy

The leaders representing each of the key areas will construct the overall company strategy more often than not on an annual basis with interim updates for a specific period as well as for an extended future time thereafter up to as much as three years.

The corporate strategy development and co-ordination is concerned with the definition of the issues that are corporate responsibilities. These may be in the form of the definition of the overall goals as well as the way in which the key stakeholders are integrated and managed.

Fundamental for the company's success is the need to nurture an environment wherein all employees are able to conduct their business in pleasant conditions with fair remuneration enjoying personal recognition and job security. Coupled to this will be the investment of finances across the various components and the development of synergies by the sharing and co-ordination of resources and staff across the different units across the company. The way the units will be governed, either in a centralised or decentralised format will influence the effectiveness of the sharing of resources and staff and therefore this should be considered very carefully in the formulation of the corporate strategy.

Factors which that need to be taken into account in the construction of the overall strategy will be the historical trading performance, current business trends, competitor activity, customer demographics, the growth of new emerging markets, economic trends like increasing fuel prices and interest rates, and evolving trends which can translate into new business opportunities, as is the case of procuring better value goods from off shore suppliers and initiatives like the exponential increase of on line shopping.

Using internal and external research with the evaluation of past performance will determine the budget targets, key performance goals and market penetration potential.

Out of the strategic workshop including the identification and management of the synergies between the key operating areas a corporate operational plan will be developed and disseminated to the relevant business areas to give guidance in the construction of their own individual strategies to ensure that the overall objectives of the company are met. This would include the need for shifts in retail, financial, marketing, information technology, real estate strategies, the sourcing of suppliers, logistical processes and provide individual operational plans that will ensure that the modifications and new initiatives are all catered for. Examples of changes may include action to penetrate new or better serve customer profiles, expand retail channels such as on line, to open new stores in new locations, implement innovative systems and reduce lead times. Fresh initiatives may be in the form of adding new product types, acquisitions, enhancing logistical operations and implement an innovative variation of loyalty programmes.

Brand strategy
The brand can be described as the personality of the retailer.

A considered view of the external and internal retail landscape has to be documented and understood. In order to enable this, team members in the buying groups, marketing, sourcing, technology, packaging, the store's visual team and designers will workshop the information gathered from past sales performance and take on board lessons learnt from the previous season, market share information, loyalty programme data analysis together with trends evident at global trade shows, catwalks, other retailers, suppliers, internet and social media.

From a planning perspective, the analysis of trade at the conclusion of the season which must include space productivity analysis and the modification of the merchandising targets need to be accounted for in terms of the impact on the brand. Typical examples of such aspects would be the effect on the customer profiles and the market penetration opportunities that arise, the open to buy reserve quantities to enable flexibility and impact on stock management and other key performance indicators which may need to be modified.

The task that is undertaken is the formulation of the direction of emerging trends in designs, core fabrics, colours, technical innovation and packaging, marketing communication as well as the highlighting of key global customer and lifestyle trends. These developments can be applied to the future season together with the identification of potential customer penetration opportunities which is vital in the input for the construction of the group buying strategies.

Service is very much a critical component of branding particularly where the retailer is own brand active and that if unsatisfactory service persists it will be unlikely that the operational expectations will be delivered. Experience shows again and again that excellent customer service lowers customer attrition rates, fosters positive messaging via word of mouth and with this comes significant increases in sales.

The positioning of the brand in the market place amongst all other competitors is determined by the attributes that make up the character of the product which helps to evaluate the product positioning in relation to other retailers and assist in ensuring that the right emphasis is achieved in order to maximise opportunities. It is critical that fashion retailers have a clear perception as to where they are positioned otherwise customers will become confused and will drift away to alternative contenders who give a clearer message as to what they stand for through the distinctive branding that identifies them.

The market positioning provides the customer with an awareness of the borders wherein the products fall and decree what they would expect to buy from the retailer. A prime example would be where a high fashion retailer introduces a traditional and conservative range of merchandise which would then send out a message that there is an older profile customer shopping in the store. It is therefore important that when a retailer consciously makes changes whether it be style, price or new ranges to reposition themselves that this intention is clearly communicated through appropriate marketing channels to the customer. Failure to do so effectively could result in them running the risk of significant write downs.

The positioning of the brand in the market is best communicated to the customer by building a marketing mix matrix which will be perceived and understood by the customers and will also facilitate benchmarks as points of reference for the retailer to compare with competitors. Distinctive branding is achieved through precise marketing, commendable public relations, a sound corporate identity and consistent messaging and image building through consistent advertising.

In the illustration below the attributes are positioned on the varying extreme scales of fashionability and value in the market and serves as a check for the retailer to ensure that they are best catering for their target customer profile by ticking off the qualities that suitably represent their products

A brand positioning model in the market can be illustrated as follows

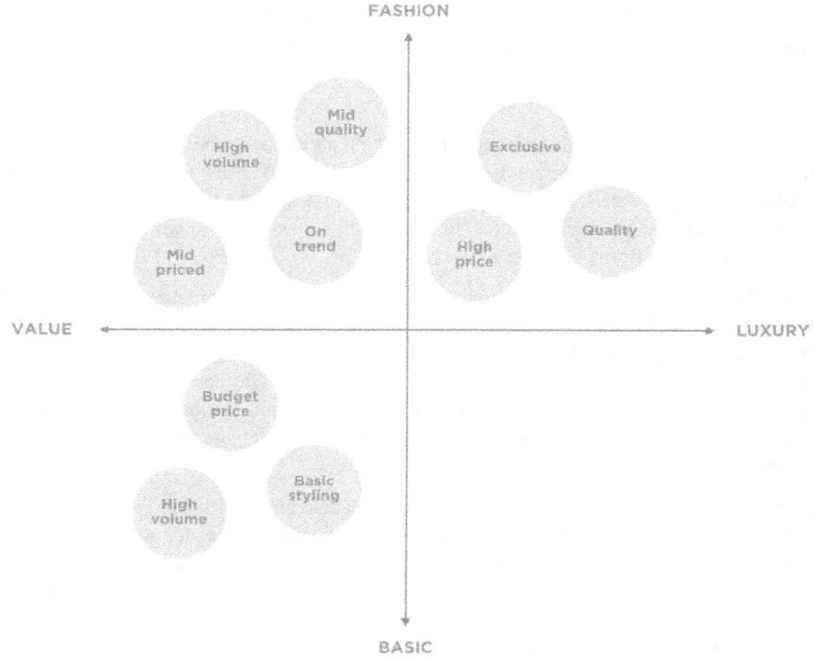

Buying group strategy

The buying group is a strategic business unit which as a profit centre can be planned independently and are less about the co-ordination of operating units but are more focused on the development and sustaining a competitive advantage for the goods that are put on offer for sale.

The formulation of the strategy is therefore more focussed on the positioning of the group against the rivals, the anticipation of the changes in demand and innovating competitive advantages such as the creation of new distribution channels or pursuing new technologies, improving product differentiation and streamlining the manufacturing processes.

Utilising the total company strategy as an input into the buying group strategy for the season will ensure that they stay aligned to the higher level objectives. The similar focus points will be considered and interpreted as they pertain to the specific buying group. Customer and trend direction must be adapted accordingly and the financial budgets, product mix of the group will need to be reviewed as a result. For the six month season period which may be split into sub seasonal periods, for example the six month winter period may well consist of a transitional three month autumn period and a high season winter time.

The trading performance and lessons learnt from the previous season as well as the customer penetration opportunities together with the competitor activity and economic landscape has to be assessed. Adjustments to the targets of the key performance measurements may have to be made to align the strategy. The customer profile relating to lifestyle and the trend forecast for the specific target market pertaining to the specific business unit will be analysed as will the financial budgets and import versus local procurement.

The strategy has to be tested against the other supporting stakeholders such as logistics, marketing, IT initiatives, human resources, trend sourcing plans and packaging revisions to ensure that these will accommodate the buying group vision.

IT initiatives may have to be reassessed to ensure that they are robust enough to meet the basic requirements that the newer applications demand in terms of response times, storage capacities, design flexibility and ease of integration with other platforms. Many such systems are able to integrate with other supporting IT applications such as supplier performance, technological measurement, critical path management, ordering, logistical and store systems.

Organisational hierarchical design must be guided by human resource expertise to enable the most efficient structures that will deliver the end in mind objectives.

A characteristic merchandise hierarchical organisational structure of a retailer is illustrated below where the mainstream buying and merchandising function cascades down from the highest platform to the lower department level details. Service areas as depicted on the right hand side of the diagram support the core functions.

Typical buying group organisation chart

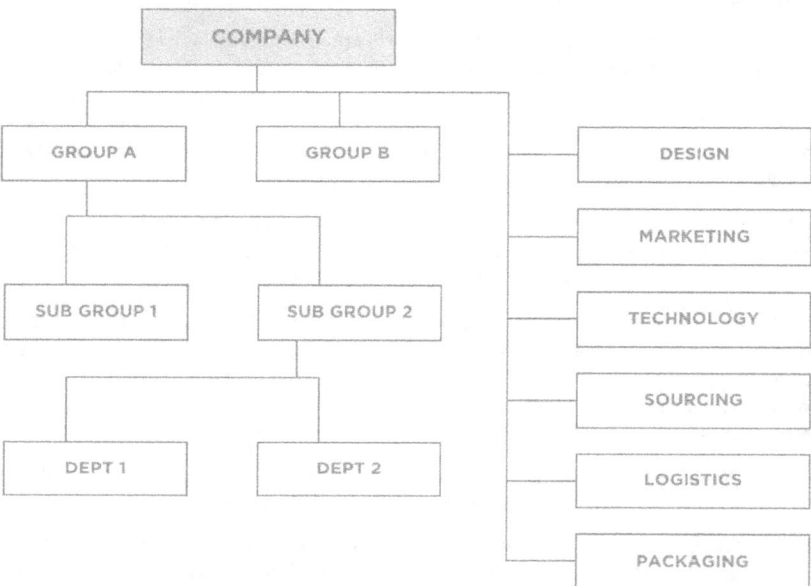

The basic hierarchical staffing roles of all the key players in a mainstream buying structure is outlined diagrammatically below.

The chief executive officer is clearly the leader together with the board of directors who ensure that the overall company strategic intent is delivered and the profits are achieved as reward to the shareholders to whom they are accountable.

Group executives look after the broad category types such as menswear, ladieswear and childrenswear. The responsibility is to ensure that the group delivers to the set strategy and is reacting properly to changing trading conditions while still meeting the profit objective.

Within the mainstream groups such as menswear a sub division into sub groups may well take place probably by lifestyle like formal wear and casual wear. The category manager is responsible for the mini business or sub group with set turnover targets, profit objectives and strategies.

Buyers, merchandisers and location planners operate at the departmental level down to the lowest degree of product being colour and size and are responsible that the management of the detail delivers the eventual goals at all the higher levels.

It must be emphasised that there is a very definitive collaborative process between the buying and merchandising team where an appropriate measure of tension may exist. The same environment may apply between the finance departments and the buying team in terms of the financial budget.

Key staffing hierarchy posts of a buying organisation

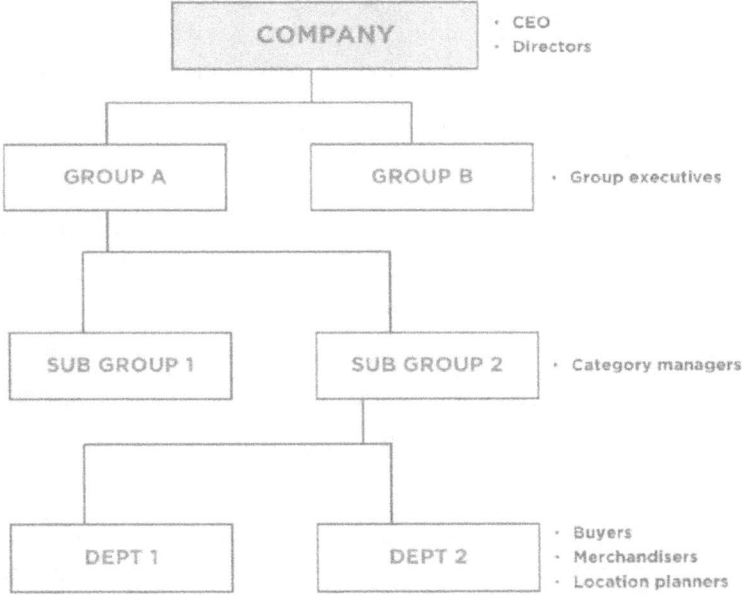

The differentiation between the key players of the procurement team in the buying group business can be broadly described as follows

Designers

Designers have a deep insight into the market they are targeting through the analysis of the changing trends and use these to provide creative direction and develop product designs for the buying teams to consider.

Usually these participants tend to think out of the box and their creative minds can challenge some of the comfort zones of other team members. What must be kept top of mind is that they need to consistently apply their intellect way ahead of time as to what they think the customer requires as opposed to their personal desires.

Typically the character traits which they will possess are that they are independent, spontaneous, extroverts, driven by ideas and are confident by nature.

Although the general perception of the word "designer" conjures up a vision of those who work at couture level, the reality is that it also includes those who are involved in creating ranges which may also be exclusive but will be more widely available and therefore can be considered as having been mass produced. Their choices will be influenced by the type of retailer they work for or the product category that they design for. The more traditional retailer which serves predominantly mature customers will be less influenced by radical fashion swings which in contrast will definitely affect the younger market's high fashion boutiques more rigorously.

Work is done at times under enormous pressure to meet critical deadlines, tough meeting schedules and involves frequent international travel. It is not surprising the perception is often one that they live a life of glory and glamour but contrary to this belief the reality is that it is not as extravagant as made out to be.

The fashion and trade shows, whether they be for yarn, fabric or garments are tiring affairs requiring hard work and stamina as is the shopping for appropriate samples, researching fashion magazines, the use of forecasting trend agencies, internet and blogs and out of all of this they need to possess the ability to then distil the emerging trends to create a storybook that will best suit their organisation's customer profiles.

The designer lives with the constant strain of knowing that their level of success will be measured by the eventual amount of money rung up at the till and getting the styling direction wrong or overextending the life of a particular look could have severe financial implications, especially in the cases where volumes are high.

The real challenge is to convince the buying teams and senior management to buy into their vision and have the confidence that what they have in mind will be commercially acceptable to the customer. The designer cannot ignore the technical aspects of the garment production as many problems can be evaded if these are taken cognisance of during the design process.

Buyers

The buyer needs to have a clear understanding of the product that is required which is in line with the trend guidelines best suited to their target customer profiles, for both the high fashion segment as well as those that best serve the more traditional customer.

It is a fact is that the role of the designer and the buyer may be a bit blurred in that they research the same fashion forecasting sites and other sources of inspiration in order to put a range of garments together. Both roles must be aware of sizing, quality and costs related to fabrics, trimmings and production. To achieve this successfully they must be flexible enough to develop and buy the most suitable product that is in line with the prescribed strategy and achieves the desired profit margin in keeping with the set down targets. The evaluation of competitive activity and product ranges through regular store visits and comparative shopping provides the knowledge required to keep ahead of the field.

Effective communication and presentation skills are a prerequisite to brief and interact with suppliers as well as presenting product reviews to colleagues within their own group at all levels of seniority. With this comes the need to be able to accept criticism and resolve problems in a mature manner. The sad fact is that frequently when the analysis of the success of the range is evaluated at the end of the season, if the results are disappointing it is not uncommon for the buyer to shoulder the emotional burden of the poor performance. The truth of the matter is that the range was presented on more than one occasion to all team players including senior management all of whom signed the range off but in the final analysis they are more often than not, as is human nature, reluctant to be accept any proper accountability.

Coupled to ability to understand the wants of the customer is the sourcing of the most suitable supplier that will be selected for the specified product types in terms of their particular skills, technical ability, costing efficiency, attitude, transparency, honesty, focus on quality, communications and competitiveness while still meeting the ethical criteria that are acceptable to society.

A large part of the task will be to maintain good relations with suppliers, while at the same time being able to assertively negotiate prices with them and make sure the planned stocks are delivered on time. Communications need to be clear and specific to avoid disputes over issues which may arise through vague and confusing messages. For these reasons they need to be confident, take decisions based on results and be driven by a sense of urgency.

The buyer has to be multi-talented in that as well as being creative they also need to monitor the sales objectively and be flexible enough to react accordingly in terms of turning on or turning off production and transferring fabric and components to more appealing product styles where sales performance and fast emerging trends dictate.

What is key to be a successful buyer is the ability to work as part of the overall team and influence the rest of the team's activities which could be in the form of a managerial and developmental capacity that could also include both their peers and superiors.

The display of emotional maturity and commercial acumen within the controlled parameters as set by the merchandising arm in terms of the budgets, the number of product options and display space constraints is absolutely essential.

The same principle applies to the relationships that need to be maintained with the technical teams in regard to the use of the most appropriate fabrics which meet the product form and function demands in addition to ensuring that the brand standards of the garment are observed.

The fact that potentially the buyer together with the other retail players will be dealing with three to four seasons simultaneously at different stages for each season makes their task even more complicated.

The ability to absorb and interpret vast amounts of information from various sources, much of which originates from complex IT systems, can present a challenge to those who are not analytically minded. Systems have altered the scope of the traditional buyer from being a pure "touchy feely art skill" to having to develop basic technical abilities through the continual emergence of innovative systems which have become a great advantage to the role.

Merchandisers

The merchandiser or planner applies their focus on maximising profitability from the business end. This is done largely through the analysis of historical sales and the influence of the trend direction to determine the range categories and product breakdown within the overall sales budget.

The role defines what stock levels are required to meet the preset targets such as seasonal stock turnover or forward stock covers based on the sales trends over time. Knowing these requirements, the merchandiser will determine what intake or purchase quantities are needed at any point in time in the season for the total department and each product category.

The level of the budgets will determine the quantity of options in relation to styling, colour palette, size spans, pricing structure and levels of quality per category that will best service the customer for the time that the goods are expected be on offer prior to a new variety of product being introduced in line with the strategic predetermined seasonal themes.

The merchandiser's job has to be to provide guidance to the buyer to procure within the budget parameters. In short it can be described as providing the buyer with a shopping list or range plan that allows them to go out and fill in the blanks on the plan while buying product. This activity requires the careful management of the "open to buy" which can often be a source of tension between the buyer who always tends to want more and the merchandiser who holds the purse strings. A good deal of emotional maturity and teamwork on both sides is therefore critical for a successful partnership.

Sadly the merchandising role is often branded as a dull, boring number crunching task in accordance with mathematical calculations and while it is this, it can be better described as a creative manipulation of numbers. This task is highly rewarding when positive trade results are achieved or alternatively equally as depressing when these do not materialise. The role can be likened to that of a husband who places his entire salary on a dead cert horse at the races which was by no means appreciated by his wife. However when the horse won he was similarly unpopular for not putting more money on the horse!

Like the buying role, the merchandiser deals with different activities simultaneously as part of the team across a number of seasons and therefore requires high levels of multi-tasking and re-prioritising in the forward planning, problem resolution, critical milestone management, analysis and timeous action implementation.

As the actual trade takes place the results need to be carefully analysed and immediate action plans initiated in order to maximise the opportunities and minimise the levels of markdowns that erode the profits. For these reasons they need to be logical, reliable, and consistent in order to take decisions based on fact.

A detailed understanding is necessary of the stores and the customer profile inherent to respective stores that are best met through the attributes of the ranges in terms of styling, colour and size that are put on offer within the store space constraints. The task is best described by the saying "plan each store as if it is your own" which could never be truer.

With sophisticated IT development and the availability of various software packages, some of which may be developed exclusively for the retailer, will provide quick sales analysis, production planning and afford the ability to make sound decisions based on accurate data. This information is especially necessary to give guidance to the allocator or distributor who will be sending the appropriate quantities to satisfy the store's needs as well as give direction as to the level of repeat buys for products that are trading above expectations.

Some organisational structures do differentiate the allocation function between the merchandiser who focuses on the forecasting and production planning and that of the allocator or location planner who will be responsible to distribute the product to the stores in the most appropriate combinations of styles, colour and sizes that meet the store profiles. This function can be housed as an extension within the buying division or may be part of a separate centralised group where an allocator may be responsible for a diverse number of departments. The benefits of such a centralised structure is that there could be a cost saving advantage especially where smaller departments do not warrant a dedicated staff member but added to this is a pool of knowledge which develops a highly skilled team who are able to cross pollinate information, coordinate inter departmental promotions effectively and develop consistent techniques and skills. The identification of common emerging trends will contribute to the optimisation of sales and assist in the control of stock quantities at a very detailed level and thereby maximise profits. Close connections to the departmental merchandisers is maintained to ensure that their actions are aligned to the departmental strategy and plans.

The need for the diversification of the function also makes more sense from the point of view in that where the distribution function is retained within the department it inevitably adds to the increasing workload of the merchandiser. The departmental merchandiser task has more and more been impacted on by the development, the implementation and mastering of complex and sophisticated information systems that analyse sales and stock with added forward planning functionalities.

Many such systems are able to integrate with other supporting IT platforms such as supplier performance, technological measurement, critical path management, ordering, logistical and store systems. The added management of a complex allocation system that is necessary to move the stock to stores is more and more difficult with the result that the incumbent is in danger of being drawn into concentrating on and coping with the intricate detail. As a result, the merchandiser runs the risk of losing sight of the bigger objectives as set out in the strategy and operational plans and the consequent degrading of the inherent merchant intuition becomes very real.

The role ensures cohesion of activities that have to be synchronized based on actual sales performance through the formalised interaction with other stakeholders such as the buyers and technologists. This contact is usually in the form of regular, typically weekly, departmental meetings where corrective decisions and plans of action are agreed. Frequent association with the points of sale in stores through written communications and reports as well as formal site visits are critical to keep aligned with the customer's preferences and emerging trends and confirm that the stores are sharing the same vision of the overall strategy.

The need to guide suppliers assertively in terms of prioritisation and the achievement of deadlines is critical to meet the suitable stock requirements at any point in time, particularly in relation to peak seasonal periods or key events. For example, once winter breaks, which it does every year except the exact date is not easy to predict, the objective is to have the right stocks in place such as knitwear, thermal underwear, scarves and the like in sufficient quantities to meet the rush. The usual manner to assist in the anticipation of the weather trend is done through reference to previous years data when the weather changes happened which also help to understand variations in out of ordinary performance at particular times. The challenge is therefore to have the appropriate quantities in the stores at the vital time while the maintenance of the balance of stocks must be adequate to cater for the demand without overstocking the stores ahead of planned stock targets. Events such as Easter, Christmas, Valentine's Day and Mother's day are easier to predict and the right levels of stock can be made more accurately available at the right time.

Where suppliers do not meet the required delivery dates, the merchandiser needs to manage the consequences that have to be applied for the underperformance. This can result in some very sensitive and emotional discussions and the negotiation of penalties typically in the form of discounts, sale or return agreements or even total cancellation which will no doubt impact negatively on both parties.

Customer strategy

Assuming that your customers are all the same is possibly the biggest error that could be made and the crucial part of growing any business is knowing intimately who your customers actually are.

Understanding the profile and lifestyle of the consumer very well is key to determine that the most appropriate product is developed to cater for the relevant customer segments and to ensure that the product information is effectively communicated through an integrated marketing plan and packaging policy.

Various factors have an influence on the profile of customers and knowledge of these will assist in the categorisation of customers and apply the most fitting methodologies that are a prerequisite to best serve them. Generally the typical segmentation of customers is determined by their behavioural needs, psychological characteristics and the environment wherein they exist. The strategic objective is to provide the customer with products that have a combination of integrity, quality and service, represent great value and create an enjoyable shopping experience in a pleasant environment that best suits the target market.

The key factors that influence the customer profiles are

BEHAVIOURAL

· Expectations of product performance
· Occasion or event purchase
· Buying habits

PSYCHOLOGICAL

· Lifestyle and income bracket
· Personality
· Image and status desirability

ENVIRONMENTAL

· Demographics of physical location
· Socio-economic composition
· Geographic location

Behavioural influences are those that in the main are habitual and accommodate the personality traits of the customer. The motivating factor for making a purchase can be varied. A consumer may not be too influenced by the on trend level of the product but will possibly prefer to have an offering that will be durable, practical and functional. If these expectations are not met they will no doubt reject the product whereas at the other end of the scale these factors may be of lesser importance.

The potential customer could be more influenced by that which is socially acceptable and reflected in the media such as magazines, television and exhibited by role models like sports stars, actors and professional people who will play an important part of the selection process. The perception of fashion could differ considerably and therefore the fashion retailer will have to rely more and more heavily on practices that will assist in analysing their particular customer's profiles or that which characterises them more accurately.

Other behaviour traits possibly are where purchases are infrequent and will exist based on a need that a shopping experience will be more of a special assignment to acquire appropriate clothing for special occasions such as returning to work, weddings, holidays or sports events.

Buying habits may include the infrequent visit to stores in order to replace the entire wardrobe on a seasonal basis in order to remain relevant and replace those clothes that have reached their performance expiry date.

The satisfaction of psychological needs such as status and image is a strong motivator in the selection of the styles that will help to achieve this objective. Included will be the perceived expectation that needs to be met by the social circle in which the purchaser moves or reflects a level of wealth that is enjoyed.

There might be the natural drive to exploit the best bargains available and some shoppers may even develop a hobby out of pursuing the greatest values available at a maze of factory and value outlets.

Trawling the glitzy malls and frequenting coffee shops and eateries can be the past time that successfully satisfies the social interaction compulsion.

The more down to earth factors that influence the shopping patterns can be the geographical location where the customer resides. As an example is that a definite difference is detected in style preference between the urbanized to those who live in remoter places where the differing demographics have a probable direct relationship to the social economic environment particularly in terms of gender, occupation, age emphasis, household income and life stage.

With the advance of till technology and the introduction of loyalty programmes it is now possible to gather a wealth of information that describes purchasing behaviour. The information that is harvested is the details of the product purchase such as style, colour, size, fit and price. The frequency and time of purchase and the relationship to other purchases can be analysed as well as the determination of the average spend per customer in different geographical areas is invaluable in building the profile of the customer base. What is of particular importance is the ability to assess the success of promotional launches and the impact they may have on other products during the time of the promotion.

There are some fundamental factors that need to be considered in terms of the population composition which needs to be taken into account in the longer term. A prime example is the greater number of older people who are still economically active at a much riper age. This is evident especially in the case of those individuals who were born at end of World War II when there was a significant baby boom and those babies are now embarking on their so called twilight years. With improved medical technology, healthier eating and lifestyles together with the explosion of health clubs as well as the trend to extend the years of economic activity has had the effect that the twilight years are going to be somewhat longer than in the past.

Another key factor is that the post war boomers enjoyed the availability of easy credit and a large number have accumulated high levels of debt with the result that when they should have been saving for their retirement years and reducing mortgages instead are landed in the situation that retirement is delayed or even worse some will have to continue working until their last.

Forensic auditing studies on mortality rate (SALT Table 1 – 1984-1986} compared in the National English tables for the period 2011 to 2013 showed that the mortality rate improved by 2.5% and 1.9% per annum for men and women respectively. Therefore the assumption can be drawn that a similar improvement going forward is likely to lie at least between these two extremes.

The impact on retailers is the need to make provision to accommodate the active aged in their store design. Store layouts will be required that are easy to shop with minimal confusion, lighting has to be bright and colour corrected to account for failing vision, noise levels need to be reduced to cater for the increased use of hearing aids, product weights must be considered and include an increased carry out service, font sizes need to be larger, shelf heights will have to be such to minimize bending and reaching while packaging should make for easier carrying and opening, queuing philosophies should be reviewed as well as the fitting rooms to permit the comfortable trying on of garments.

At the other end of the scale, the younger generations typically born in the seventies and eighties known as the millennial generation or generation Y are evolving into an extremely different personality to their predecessors and have become legendry in their prolific spending, their brand awareness and because they are technologically advanced this makes them more adventurous. Such characteristics may be evident in the pursuit of their career aspirations as they tend to progress through various places of employment while carving their career at a whim in contrast to their parents who often followed the same occupation for a lifetime. Because these cool, energetic participants are screen junkies they are easily influenced by social media trends and fads. They are therefore able to make informed comparisons and as a result the loyal practice of only shopping at one destination is almost non-existent which places a real test on the retailers to capture a core base market.

Marketing is left with an incredible task to innovate and communicate with this new breed of customer that is arriving on the scene at a rapid pace. Retailers have to start thinking like their customers as in place of window shopping this new breed trawls the internet and stays in contact all the time via the social channels and consequently the retailer need to ramp up their image amongst the channels through financial investment in top class copy writing and superb photographs as well as actively interact on line with their customer. The location of the on line sites should, as with bricks and mortar outlets, be in the best possible space where the greatest exposure to the target customer through the measurement of the number of click troughs is achieved. The offering must be easily found on websites that are advertised forcefully among local advertising vehicles, public relations efforts, promotions and word of mouth.

A popular trend emerging amongst digital enthusiasts is the support for blog sites where the brands are able to speak to an audience in a different light. There is a word of caution in that what they tell the people must be well accepted because should it be met with resistance the consequences could be equally disastrous. Examples exist of some successful fashion blogs that attract thirty thousand hits a day and may have up to two hundred thousand followers on twitter and therefore brands are happy to pay a lot of money to purchase advertising space in these forums. Some brands spend more than fifty percent of their advertising provision on electronic channels and collaborate with bloggers to gain the most editorial exposure. Many designers view the bloggers as their spokespersons as they develop strong relationships with customers by offering fashion tips and advice, the provision of educational material and programmes that help with the customer decision making process as well as at the same time enhancing brand awareness.

Product planning strategy

Once there is a clear understanding of what operational activities are required, the plan of action can be outlined to deliver the strategic objectives and thereby satisfy the goals of the strategy in the most effective way.

What is key in formulating the planning strategy is to set down the clear guidelines in the development of the product mix which will be carefully tailored in the right proportions in order to best serve the customer at the various locations and in terms of styling, colour quantities across the sizes at the most acceptable prices.

For this to be done successfully the overall process of planning follows a set of prescribed activities that make up the mechanics of running the business as well as accommodating the other stakeholder strategies. The steps are a flow of taking in the lessons learnt during the previous season and utilising the learnings as input in the formulation of the strategic goals for the future season.

The goals will give guidance in the preparation of the level of budgets determining the product mix and setting up the range plan from which the orders will be placed. Once production has taken place according to the plan the goods will be allocated to the stores taking into account their specific customer characteristics. Sales will be analysed as they occur and as the performance dictates the forward plans will be reviewed and adjusted appropriately.

Diagrammatically the high level key planning steps can be outlined as follows

Believe it or not the start of planning for a forthcoming season begins with what has happened in the past.

A strategic focus in the assessment of the past performance for the season is to compare the actual vital numbers to that what was expected and understand the deviations whether they were positive or negative. The learnings are imperative in the compilation of a new season's strategy and the setting of targets.

Planning strategy

Once there is a clear understanding of what operational activities are required, the plan of action can be outlined to deliver the strategic objectives and thereby satisfy the goals of the strategy in the most effective way.

What is key in formulating the planning strategy is to set down the clear guidelines in the development of the product mix which will be carefully tailored in the right proportions in order to best serve the customer at the various locations and in terms of styling, colour quantities across the sizes at the most acceptable prices.

For this to be done successfully the overall process of planning follows a set of prescribed activities that make up the mechanics of running the business as well as accommodating the other stakeholder strategies. The steps are a flow of taking in the lessons learnt during the previous season and utilising the learnings as input in the formulation of the strategic goals for the future season.

The goals will give guidance in the preparation of the level of budgets determining the product mix and setting up the range plan from which the orders will be placed. Once production has taken place according to the plan the goods will be allocated to the stores taking into account their specific customer characteristics. Sales will be analysed as they occur and as the performance dictates the forward plans will be reviewed and adjusted appropriately.

Process

In conjunction with the buyers, designers, sourcing specialists and the technologists, the merchandise planner is responsible for the delivery of the departmental strategy to make sure it is aligned to the strategic intent of the company and the group.

The sales estimation and the planning of the stock levels are done to achieve the sales and margin objectives from departmental level down to the individual product level. Together with the buyer the range planning and building will take place to construct a complete balanced offer of product that satisfies the needs of the target customers.

The construction of a range plan may commence once the financial targets are available through the product and store plans together with a store catalogue matrix. The range plan enables the drafting of a so called "shopping list" for the buying team to be able to fill in the blanks as they make their selections.

Prior to the building of the range or buying plan there must be an indication of the expected item sales in money value and units as well as the relative proportion splits across the range for the various store catalogues with the relative variances between this year and last year for the sales value, units and price which will all serve as the preliminary basis for discussion and provide the guidance for the formulation of the intake and range flow plan.

An example of a line by line summary is as follows

PROD NO	DESCRIPTION	STORE CATALOGUE	SELLING PRICE			SALES '000			SALES UNITS		
			LY	TY	% inc/dec	LY	TY	% inc/dec	LY	TY	% inc/dec
	PROD GROUP 1										
1001	Style ABCD	All	95.00	99.99	5.2%	680 000	730 000	5.7%	7 158	7 300	2.0%
2001	Style ABCE	All	125.00	129.99	4.0%	500 000	550 000	10.0%	4 000	4 231	5.7%
	PROD GROUP 2										
1002	Style ABCF	All	175.00	180.00	2.9%	299 000	350 000	17.0%	1 708	1 944	13.8%
2002	Style ABCG	All	175.00	180.00	2.9%	345 000	400 000	15.9%	1 971	2 222	12.8%
3001	Style ABCH	All	175.00	180.00	2.9%	365 000	390 000	6.8%	2 085	2 027	9.7%
TOTAL DEPARTMENT			129.40	136.53	5.5%	2 189 000	2 420 000	10.6%	16 922	17 724	4.7%

Building the flow range plan

The purpose of the range plan is to ensure that the offer of commercial and all-inclusive product ranges meet the needs of all customers. This is done through the combination of the elements of science which covers the planning aspect and art that represents the buying function. To expand further, the scientific practice delivers the clarity of the range offer, the quantities of style and colour levels with the correct pricing policies that support structured cataloguing which meet the varying customer profile pools. The artistic involvement delivers beautiful product and style in categories offering real choice in a way that they are easy to shop. The determination to achieve a successful balanced combination will assist in the potential maximisation of sales and profit as well as undoubtedly help to grow market share.

The philosophies of building a range is the procedure of analysing the historical sales of product categories as well as heeding the lessons learnt from previous seasons and being guided by the strategic definitions. Modifications to the current range structures could be done to compensate for missed opportunities, lost sales through uncommon adversities should be accounted for as is the need to cater for inflated sales as a result of upcoming out of the norm special events.

A balance of the right product mix between the basic range types and the fashion inputs has to be determined. The large volume items should be the first focus to ensure that the relevant high money takers are looked after adequately. Second is the necessity to correctly identify the characteristics of fashion forward goods for each product category in order that they best meet the respective store groupings customer profiles and reflect good relative value to other internal or external products.

A simple range plan model based on the guidelines reflected in the departmental line summary above is illustrated as follows.

Department XYZ Range Plan

Product Group	Style	Colour	Stores	Cont /input	Cost price	Sell price	Intake margin	Intake sell value	Intake units	Month 1 Week 1	Week 2	Week 3	Week 4	Week 5	Month 2 Week 6	Week 7	Week 8	Month 3 Week 9	Week 10	Week 11	Week 12	Week 13
1																						
1001	White	All	Cont	46.99	99.99	53%	2500000	25020	150	175	200	225	175	175	200	275	160	200	175	175	250
	Black	All	Cont	46.99	99.99	53%	2000000	2000	120	140	160	160	100	140	200	270	120	160	140	140	200
	Blue	Grp A,B,C	Cont	46.99	99.99	53%	1900000	9600	96	112	128	144	80	112	128	178	96	128	112	112	160
	Purple	Grp A,B	Cont	46.99	99.99	53%	120000	1200	72	84	96	108	60	84	96	132	96	96	84	84	120
2001	Beige	All	Cont	63.69	129.99	51%	3000000	23108	138	162	185	208	155	162	185	186	185	185	162	162	231
	White	All	Cont	63.69	129.99	51%	2500000	1923	115	135	154	173	96	135	202	216	154	154	135	182	192
	Green	Grp A	Cont	63.69	129.99	51%	100000	769	46	46	54	61	38	61	64	84	46	61	54		77
Product group 1				Intake units					12500													
				Merchandise intake value			13380000	13960500		738	985	981	1107	835	981	1153	738	984	984	984	1250	
										829150	909600	1104400	1241100	693000	1104400	1104400	839350	1104400	1104400	966200		
										829150	966135	1140465	1242145	834525	966135	1158305	839350	1104440	1104440	966135	1380450	
2																						
1702	Purple	All	Input	82.81	180	54%	1380000	12500	738												
1703	Yellow	All	Input	82.81	180	54%	120000	833	736	865	575	1107	635	863	1153	788	984	984	861	1250
	Orange	Grp A,B	Input	82.81	180	54%	80000	667	963		100										
2002	Pink	All	Input	82.81	180	54%	170000	444	378		67		833		142	997				
	Brown	All	Input	82.81	180	54%	140000	944					661		137	803				
	Black	Grp A,B	Input	82.81	180	54%	900000	778					472		63	614				
3001	Green	All	Input	82.81	180	54%	900000	556												
	White	All	Input	82.81	180	54%	170000	1066												
	Grey	Grp A,B	Input	82.81	180	54%	1300000	944												
Product group 2				Intake units					69444													
				Intake selling value			12500000	12500000	1651	2975600		590	52600	8336		342	3314		4508		
				Merchandise intake plan						2975600	929500	929500	3485000	619500	4185000	235500	4185000	735400			
3																						
1003	Purple	All	Input	103.42	220	53%	190000	682	580	580	103	657		555		1854	328			
2003	Yellow	All	Input	103.42	220	53%	190000	775	657	186		657		186		647	116			
	Orange	Grp A,B	Input	103.42	220	53%	120000	546	464	82		754		150		902	89			
	Pink	All	Input	103.42	220	53%	170000	773				502		89		695	131			
3002	Brown	All	Input	103.42	220	53%	190000	864								803	116			
	Black	Grp A,B	Input	103.42	220	53%	180000	591								902	89			
	Green	All	Input	103.42	220	53%	170000	808												
	White	All	Input	103.42	220	53%	150000	783												
	Grey	Grp A	Input	103.42	220	53%	150000	591												
Product group 3				Intake units					8411													
				Intake selling value			3410000		1701	37.4230	500	1107	1895		355	1353	1854	328		
				Merchandise intake plan				1410000	374090	374090	65000	124700	416500		73950	153900	408000	72000		
										374090	653820	124245	416860		73480	153855	408020	72600		
Total Dept XYZ				Intake units					25655													
				Intake selling value			45000000		4292	861	5573	1107	4444	860	1353	49006	984	1720		
				Merchandise intake plan			45010700	149200	7545310	966600	2279060	1247200	8340000	966600	1853800	9073200	180400	258900		
										7544440	966135	2287760	1242145	8314525	966135	2454490	907250	180440	258544		

For clarification of the range plan section A provides all the key data of the product in terms of product group in terms of the department's product group, style, colour, sore catalogue, whether the style is a fashion input or is a replenishment continuity line, the cost and selling price as well the resultant intake margin. The total intake value and intake units represents the "buy".

The intake value and unit buy is summarised at the product group and total level with a comparison to the merchandise intake plan which delivers the alignment status between the assortment plan and the merchandise financial plan.

Section A

Department XYZ Range Plan

Product Group	Style	Colour	Stores	Cont /input	Cost price	Sell price	Intake margin	Intake sell value	Intake units
1	1001	White	All	Cont	46.99	99.99	53%	250000	2500
		Black	All	Cont	46.99	99.99	53%	200000	2000
		Blue	Grp A,B,C	Cont	46.99	99.99	53%	160000	1600
		Purple	Grp A,B	Cont	46.99	99.99	53%	120000	1200
	2001	Beige	All	Cont	63.69	129.99	51%	300000	2308
		White	All	Cont	63.69	129.99	51%	250000	1923
		Green	Grp A	Cont	63.69	129.99	51%	100000	768
Product group 1			Intake units						12300
			Intake selling value					1380000	
			Merchandise intake plan					1380500	
2	1002	Purple	All	Input	82.81	180	54%	150000	833
		Yellow	All	Input	82.81	180	54%	120000	667
		Orange	Grp A,B	Input	82.81	180	54%	80000	444
	2002	Pink	All	Input	82.81	180	54%	170000	944
		Brown	All	Input	82.81	180	54%	140000	778
		Black	Grp A,B	Input	82.81	180	54%	100000	556
	3001	Green	All	Input	82.81	180	54%	190000	1056
		White	All	Input	82.81	180	54%	170000	944
		Grey	Grp A,B	Input	82.81	180	54%	130000	722
Product group 2			Intake units						6944
			Intake selling value					1250000	
			Merchandise intake plan					1250100	
3	1003	Purpl	All	Input	103.42	220	53%	150000	682
		Yellow	All	Input	103.42	220	53%	170000	773
		Orange	Grp A,B	Input	103.42	220	53%	120000	546
	2003	Pink	All	Input	103.42	220	53%	170000	773
		Brown	All	Input	103.42	220	53%	190000	864
		Black	Grp A,B	Input	103.42	220	53%	130000	591
	3002	Green	All	Input	103.42	220	53%	180000	808
		White	All	Input	103.42	220	53%	170000	783
		Grey	Grp A,B	Input	103.42	220	53%	130000	591
Product group 3			Intake units						6411
			Intake selling value					1410000	
			Merchandise intake plan					1410100	
Total Dept XYZ			Intake units						25655
			Intake selling value					4040000	
			Merchandise intake plan					4040700	

Section B represents the monthly and weekly intake required across time in the same or similar shape as the merchandise intake plan in units per style in units which represent the quantities that will be required to be contracted and reflected on the production plans of the relevant suppliers.

The total values are summarised in units, intake value and relationship to the financial merchandise intake plan by month and week

Section B

	Month 1				Month 2				Month 3				
week 1	week 2	week 3	week 4	week 5	week 6	week 7	week 8	week 9	week 10	week 11	week 12	week 13
150	175	200	225	125	175	200	275	150	200	200	175	250
120	140	160	180	100	140	160	220	120	160	160	140	200
96	112	128	144	80	112	128	176	96	128	128	112	160
72	84	96	108	60	84	96	132	72	96	96	84	120
138	162	185	208	115	162	185	254	136	185	185	162	231
115	135	154	173	96	135	154	212	115	154	154	135	192
46	46	54	61	38	54	61	84	46	61	61	54	77
738	861	981	1107	615	861	981	1353	738	984	984	861	1230
82800	96600	110400	124200	69000	96600	110400	151800	82800	110400	110400	96600	138000
82830	96635	110440	124245	69025	96635	110440	151855	82830	110440	11044	96635	138050
708		125										
567		100										
378		67										
				803		142						
				661		117						
				472		83						
								897		158		
								803		142		
								614		108		
1853		292		1938		342		2314		408		
297500		52500		348500		61500		416500		73500		
297600		52400		348700		61600		416400		73400		
580		102										
657		116										
464		82										
				657		116						
				734		130						
				502		89						
								685		123		
								667		116		
								502		89		
1701		300		1993		335		1854		328		
374220		65000		416500		73500		408000		72000		
374010		65920		416800		73450		408020		72100		
4292	861	1573	1107	4444	861	1658	1353	4906	984	1720		
754520	96600	227900	124200	834000	96600	245400	151800	907300	110400	255900		
754440	96635	228760	124245	834525	96635	245490	151855	907250	110440	158544		

The creation of the initial range plan reflects the quantities that have to be bought at individual style level by colour, in the correct size ranges, at the target mark-ups and retail selling prices. It is essential that the monetary buying amounts of the plan are aligned to the merchandise plan intake values.

The buying plan should reflect the strategy which guarantees the correct amount of selection within the stock parameters while still providing the right spread of products in the required quantities that will best serve the target customer in both style, form and function at any point in time of the season.

During the construction of the plan, the principle that needs to be adhered to is that the merchandise plan must guide the buy with the customer top of mind. Lessons learnt from previous seasons need to be analysed and equally applied to both the basic continuity lines as well as the high end fashion products. Fundamentally it is also important to get the right balance of the correct number of choices in quantities that enable the guarantee of basic lines in depth without impeding the introduction of newness.

It happens often that too much emphasis is placed on the fringe or peripheral lines, or there is excessive similarity in characteristics and price offerings that can disrupt the balance. The emotional wishes of the buying team and suppliers can also have an influence on a distorted balance being achieved and should be guarded against.

The range plan which represents the assortment of products developed within specific categories must represent the organisation of the business and therefore should be balanced across the width and depth of the structure.

The width represents how broad the choice of product is while the depth represents the quantities required to cover the number of sizes and colours including the amount of price points within the product categories. It is probably easier for niche retailers that focus on a narrower customer segment of the market to best be able to serve the both the depth and width demands of their market.

The difficulties that retailers are faced with in striking the right balance of width and depth of ranges is that of presenting real customer choice while at same time optimising the return on investment. In other words, there is the need to attract customers by maintaining a level of newness and fashionability without compromising the traditional or core customers and especially the high volume sellers. It is therefore critical that the buyer has a clear vision of the marketing position and understands the target customer though continuous research which provides the confidence to determine as to what should or should not be kept in the range.

It remains a challenge to constantly balance the needs of the customer versus the cost to provide enough variety. Often the safer option seems to try and cover all bases by having a wide selection of goods which de-risk the unpredictability of demand but the downside is that the chances of high left overs at the end of the season or the life cycle of the product results in intensified write downs. At the other extreme it takes bold thinking to minimise the variety and sit with higher stocks in few styles but the risk is therefore if a style does not sell the cost of markdown could be very high and a specific need may not be satisfied at all.

A great variety of product on offer adds complexity in the decision making process which is not only frustrating and diminishes the shopping experience but leaves a higher potential of buyer's remorse after being overwhelmed by choice. It is for this reason that the retailer has a clear understanding as to who their target customer is and apply a brand positioning model accordingly to eliminate those choices that do not cater for their needs and thereby keep confusion and number of choices to a minimum.

A general tendency related to fashion retailers appears that as a rule of thumb that about fifty to sixty percent of their product is sold out during its lifecycle with the rest being sold at a discount of about thirty to fifty percent thereby resulting in a fifteen to twenty percent reduction of margin and an eventual complete write off of about five percent.

The volume and choice balance emphasis that the customer expects to find new styles in their size in a variety of colours can be illustrated as follows.

Style and shape proportions

The styles that will make up the range structure are dictated by history, the strategy guidelines and direction provided by the design or trend teams.

If one considers the thought process of a customer when a selection is being made, the first feature that she will be attracted to is the style. If the style does not meet the required taste level it will be ignored. The criteria that will influence this choice may not necessarily be the level of fashionability but also the practicality of the garment in meeting the required functionality, examples of which are sleeve lengths, belted or unbelted waists, lengths, neckline or any other feature that will allow the customer to feel comfortable and confident to wear.

Multiple choices form the basis of range plan structure and ensure that all customer preferences are catered for. Another need that has to be provided for is the availability of styling and colours that can be easily coordinated with other product styles within the same or other departments.

Consideration also needs to be given to the cross co-ordination of fashionable items being supported by core product. An example would be a fashion blouse including the core shades in the design or print that would go happily with a basic core skirt in complimentary fabric types. The implementation of this strategy is important as too much deviation from the core pillars will reduce the product relevance and could result in a deterioration of market penetration.

Pricing structure

It is absolutely essential to consider the structure or architecture of pricing across the range in order that a consistent balance is maintained between the good value, mid and luxury price points. Added to this is the controlling of the price movement from one season to the next. The rate of increases or decreases need to be measured on a like for like basis whereby the change in price of identical products is compared to an acceptable overall rate such as the consumer price index while still maintaining the margin targets. Other products should also represent good value in comparison to similar products in the market place.

The philosophy and pricing strategy of the retailer will dictate the balance of price groups dependent on the customer segments that they serve. Probable examples would be where a discount value chain will have about ninety percent of product in the low value band while the middle price type of retailer will have possibly forty percent low price goods with the bulk of products falling into the mid-price range at about fifty five percent. Top end luxury retailers will commonly have in excess of ninety percent of prices falling in the high price range.

A pitfall that needs to be avoided is a scenario where critical price points are maintained through harsh negotiation tactics for more than one or two seasons as it could happen that it will eventually reach a point that without an increase it may become no longer viable for the supplier to manufacture. A decision to then move the price to a realistic level could result in the customer resisting the purchase as a result of the perception that the price is excessive in relation to the previous season. Credibility may also be lost as there may be great difficulty in justifying the narrower gap difference between other products within the range and they in turn could be interpreted to represent poor value.

Extreme deep cut promotions may have a similar impact and the danger exists that the balance of the margins may become distorted. An overall anticipated intake margin is based on planned quantities but in reality is rapidly lessened where repetitive turn-ons of the lower margin product takes place.

A factor that must be considered is the effect of the price movement on unit volumes and whether or not the reduced quantities will still service the store catalogue sufficiently to maintain good continuity. If this is not the case it may require the rationalisation of the number of customer choices offered or a restriction of the store catalogue for the product.

A tactic that retailers frequently resort to in terms of a psychological influence is the selection of the number of price points as well as the pricing terminology. For this reason price points such as 99.00 presents a better perception of value than if the product was marked 100.00. This technique however must be handled with caution as for high ticketed items it is better to present 300.00 rather than 299.00 as this may deliver a message of perceived deviousness. In terms of the gaps between price points, the wider they are among the product groups the better is the value perception. In cases where the customer is bombarded with too many price options it becomes increasingly difficult to assess the value variance between products.

Retailers sometimes apply regional pricing where the income status of customers differ. The result is that customers in the poorer areas enjoy a discount that is subsidised by those in the more affluent areas. Similarly there are unscrupulous retailers who launch a product at an unrealistic high price and after a short period reduce it to a price that delivers a normal margin but is promoted aggressively as great value. These practices once exposed are not well received by consumers and become great topics of discussion on social media.

Colour range

The second determining feature of the product that will influence the purchasing decision will be the colour. Colour is the first element of newness and trend direction that is displayed. Many season's ranges can fail through poor interpretation of the seasonal colour trend. How the colour themes are flowed across the seasons is important as is the harmony that exists with not only the colours within each individual product range but also with the overall look of the store. The visual impact is important in that it transmits a subliminal message to the customer through a fine balance of fashion colours to those that the customer prefers.

Core colours should be banked first even though they may not always be the most exciting. A wise retailer once said "white is a business" and this certainly holds true for black, grey, navy, beige and brown year in and year out. The trending themes such as lilacs, pinks, yellows are more often than not linked to the prevailing trends and will dictate the seasonal themes from month to month. There is a place for the high risk edgy colours such funky pinks, shocking purples and burnt oranges as they provide the theatre even though they may not deliver the best returns.

In order to achieve the best variety it is important to ensure that the planned colour spectrum is reflected as a whole by assigning different colours across the diverse styles in the range with the overall proportions meeting the targets of the strategic intent.

Examining the table below it is evident that the plan is not aligned to the strategic target and therefore a revisit to the proportions will be required to bring them in line with the objective.

NUMBER	COLOUR	UNITS	LY	UNITS PLANNED	TY	TY TARGET
1	White	250	19%	356	25%	28%
2	Black	430	33%	356	25%	25%
3	Stone	130	10%	178	13%	15%
4	Khaki	200	15%	178	13%	12%
5	Red	250	19%	178	13%	10%
6	Pink	40	3%	178	13%	10%
	TOTAL	1 300	100%	1 424	100%	100%

Size architecture

As has been highlighted previously, the first attractor to the customer is the style and then colour but the reality remains that the choice will only be complete if the size is available in the wanted style and colour. For this reason many retailers will display their offerings by size so as to minimize the frustration that results when the size is not available in the desired style and colour.

The need to minimise the non-availability of particular sizes is the main reason as to why special attention should be paid to the careful planning and analysis of size profiles.

It is logical that stores have differing size profiles which are driven by the local demographics, shopping patterns and cultural preferences. For this reason the product groupings and styling features need to be carefully assessed. Typical examples would be that possibly in the rural areas customers may be genetically of a larger stature than their counterparts in the cities and could also have a more conservative attitude than the adventurous city slickers. Religious beliefs may also have an influence where certain parts of the body such as arms need to be covered.

As with the top down and bottom up merchandise planning principle we need to determine the overall national size curve for a department, product category and product in order to place the full combined order with the supplier.

Similarly the accumulated store size profiles have to be derived and aligned with the product size profile in order that allocations can meet both the product and store needs.

The size analysis for small, medium and large emphasis size stores will require differing size ratios for each group.

Once production is complete the supplier will advise via a report what volumes by size and colour are complete and packaged ready for dispatch to the addresses as stipulated by the retailer.

Allocations

Sales will never be exactly as expected as the customers do not have prior knowledge of the plans and will always buy differently. Coupled to this the amount of over or under production due to a reject factor could result in availabilities being higher or lower than what the supplier was meant to make and therefore the actual closing stock at the end of each period will definitely vary to the expectation. Markdown values are also continually different to that planned.

Let us assume that the intake plan in monetary value was previously planned as follows

	TOTAL SEASON	MONTH 1				MONTH 2				MONTH 3				
		WK 1	WK 2	WK 3	WK 4	WK 5	WK 6	WK 7	WK 8	WK 9	WK 10	WK 11	WK 12	WK 13
OPEN STOCK	77 000	77 000	79 000	82 000	81 000	81 000	88 000	96 000	98 000	98 000	99 000	98 000	91 000	83 000
SALES	370 000	10 000	12 000	14 000	14 000	12 000	13 000	14 000	15 000	13 000	14 000	19 000	21 000	16 000
MARKDOWN	700				700									
INTAKE	376 700	12 000	15 000	13 000	14 700	19 000	21 000	16 000	15 000	14 000	13 000	12 000	13 000	15 000
FWD COVER		6	6	6	6	6	6	6	6	6	6	6	6	6
CLOSING STOCK	83 000	79 000	82 000	81 000	81 000	88 000	96 000	98 000	98 000	99 000	98 000	91 000	83 000	82 000

	TOTAL SEASON	MONTH 4				MONTH 5				MONTH 6				
		WK 14	WK 15	WK 16	WK 17	WK 18	WK 19	WK 20	WK 21	WK 22	WK 23	WK 24	WK 25	WK 26
OPEN STOCK	77 000	82 000	83 000	84 000	85 000	86 000	87 000	87 000	85 000	83 000	83 000	85 000	85 000	83 000
SALES	370 000	15 000	14 000	13 000	12 000	13 000	15 000	16 000	15 000	14 000	13 000	14 000	15 000	14 000
MARKDOWN	700													
INTAKE	376 700	16 000	15 000	14 000	13 000	14 000	15 000	14 000	13 000	14 000	15 000	14 000	13 000	14 000
FWD COVER		6	6	6	6	6	6	6	6	6	6	6	6	6
CLOSING STOCK	83 000	83 000	84 000	85 000	86 000	87 000	87 000	85 000	83 000	83 000	85 000	85 000	83 000	83 000

Stocks and sales are the anchor targets that are consistently aimed for with the intake being the balancing variable to bring the plan back in line. In the hypothetical exercise below done for Month 1 of the plan it is illustrated as to how the intake is manipulated over the four weeks of the month in order to meet the original stock targets.

Intake adjustment to reconcile to target stocks

	TOTAL SEASON	MONTH 1			
		WK 1	WK 2	WK 3	WK 4
OPEN STOCK	77 000	77 000	79 000	82 000	81 000
ACTUAL OPEN STOCK	80 000	80 000	80 300	78 800	78 800
SALES	50 000	10 000	12 000	14 000	14 000
ACTUAL SALES	45 600	7 000	10 000	14 500	14 100
MARKDOWN	700				700
ACTUAL MARKDOWN	800			200	600
INTAKE	54 700	12 000	15 000	13 000	14 700
ACTUAL INTAKE	47 400	7 300	8 500	14 700	16 900
FWD COVER		6	6	6	6
ACTUAL FWD COVER		5	5	5	5
CLOSING STOCK	83 000	79 000	82 000	81 000	81 000
ACTUAL CLOSING STOCK	81 000	80 300	78 800	78 800	81 000

To summarise for the month, the total actual monetary value of sales missed target by 4400 and due to the fact that the actual stock opened higher than expectation by 3000 with 100 more markdown then target resulted in the intake for the month having to be reduced from a plan of 54700 to 47400.

It must be noted that the monetary intake requirement needs to be converted to units at the style/colour level to enable the stock availability to be allocated and distributed.

The allocation of product from the availability reports provided by suppliers or stocks stored in the warehouse takes on two methodologies. The input type products, usually for seasonal launches or fashion styles are described as "push" products while the continuity product which is replenished in empathy to sales performance are known as "pull" products where allocations are triggered by minimum stock level points and stopped by the maximum stock level thresholds.

The key differentiators of these types of products are that "push" styles cater for peak sales before being replaced. These styles attract a higher markdown volume as they are removed off display once the range becomes broken as they need to make way for the new themes that the replacement input styles bring.

"Pull" styles determine the requirements based on replacement of actual sales to a pre-determined build to level of stock. The calculation of the quantity of stock required will be the be determined by the amount of intake needed to meet the stock target that is either dynamically determined by the set weeks sales forward cover or is maintained at a static level over time.

"Pull" styles should typically be continuity items that have a predictable rate of sale and have a balanced availability of sufficient volumes of stock from the lowest level to meet the fluctuating demand. The supplier's production planning therefore has to be consistently reliable and flexible to sustain this condition.

The "pull" principle can be illustrated as follows

STOCK
LEVEL

MAX

MIN

TIME

The automatic replenishment or distribution of products is often performed through the use of sophisticated technical allocation systems and are most suitable for the basic continuity product that have consistent predictable sales patterns and for store displays which are laid out according to a centralised space planning system.

The application needs to be merged with the historical sales data and the planned overall sales going forward. In order to achieve a constant replenishment over time a technique of smoothing is utilised where a weighting factor is applied to sales which deviate from the norm due to an unusual event and in such cases the system will use the adjusted realistic level of sale in the algorithm to derive the most appropriate forward allocations.

In the case where there is a launch of new lines, the new line can be linked to the pattern of a similar current style. The performance of the new styles must therefore be very carefully monitored early on and adjusted if need be to ensure the best size provision as possible.

The manual overriding of calculated allocations at store level should only take place in exceptional circumstances for specific reasons such as unforeseen special events, competitor activity or natural disasters. Often the temptation exists to manually override allocations based on an inherent gut feel and this should be avoided at all costs.

The delivery instruction which is sent to the supplier specifies the quantities that must be picked and packed per item per store by colour and size.

The primary size refers to the commonly designated size of all products such as waist measurements, neck and chest sizes while the secondary size refers to products which have other options of the main primary size such as different leg lengths for trousers or varying cup size options in case of bras.

If automated replenishment systems do not exist or are not very sophisticated it may occur that the actual sales by size do not mirror those as planned. In such cases it is necessary to review the size patterns using a manual technique and alter contract ratios going forward. A special balancing contract must be raised for production of those specific sizes that are short in order to realign the size sales pattern to that of the amended regular contracts going forward. A very clear indication where the size ratio is out of line is where at the end of range launches the left over stocks or reduced stocks are dominated by one or two sizes. If one applies one's mind to the consequence of this, it is a fact that potential sales have gone drastically astray of better selling sizes and profit is consequently not maximised.

In summary, the sad part about poor performers or the lack of stock control, is that especially in the case of high volume continuity styles, the resultant negative impact can be likened to a lingering illness that lives with the buying team until the situation of overstocks of unwanted product is eventually rectified or doomed to the reduced counter. It is therefore critical that where there is a hint of such an evolving scenario that very swift action is taken.

Where there has been above average performance of categories, a situation may arise where the amount stock available is unable to satisfy the requirements of the entire store catalogue. In such instances the predicament that exists is one of how to keep everybody happy. The choice usually boils down to reducing the quantities proportionately across the entire catalogue dependent on the priority of need whereby at least each store sees a piece of the pie before sell outs are experienced. The other option is to take the view to shrink the number of stores that are serviced and best satisfy the stores that are more likely to deliver the greatest volume of sales. In many cases it is not uncommon for twenty percent of the catalogue to deliver sixty to seventy percent of the sales. The selection of the second option will retain the credibility of the customers in the bigger units but will disappoint the many customers across the balance of the stores. A tactic to alleviate severe situations is by choosing a geographical cross section of stores and if an on-line facility exists, to ensure that stock is available at all times that can be ordered via the internet.

The use of digital imaging has helped develop realistic three dimensional representations which enable the product to be placed efficiently on the various types of equipment in the store. Such systems operate at detail size level so in theory a store will never be out of a size as the principle applied is that as the store sells one it gets one. The key to the success of such a system is that the data integrity has to be as accurate as possible. If this is not the case, for example, where the data base is distorted through incorrect barcode ticketing or pilferage will result in allocations being calculated inaccurately. The only means to rectify the data base is to do a disciplined full manual stock count from time to time and update the data base accordingly.

Delivery Instruction note example

ORDER NO	12345	DEPARTMENT	Men's Trousers
SUPPLIER	ABC Manufacturer	STYLE NO	5554
DATE	14 March, 2015	DESCRIPTION	Casual cotton trouser

	STORES	COLOUR	GREY					
		PRIMARY SIZE	32	34	36	38	40	42
		SECONDARY SIZE	32	34	36	38	40	42
NO	STORE	TOTAL	120	170	160	140	110	100
141	City Centre	250	38	53	50	44	34	66
145	Main Street	200	30	43	40	35	28	53
148	Back Street	250	38	53	50	44	34	66
151	Country Lane	100	15	21	20	18	14	26

The intake and orders are carefully controlled to meet the stock requirements as per the plan at any given time while the allocation and distribution of stock is managed in such a way in order to optimise the fulfilment of the customer demands within the selling space available.

Trading

No matter how much time and thought is spent in drafting the strategy and planning forecast it is inevitable that the reality will deviate from what is expected as a result of the volatile internal and external factors that exist at the time. Therefore it is critical to continually review actual performance, analyse the trends and take appropriate action to minimise the risks. Where adjustments are not able to be made to remedy a situation the lessons learnt must be taken on board and banked to be avoided in future trading seasons.

The path to follow in the process of comparing the actual performance in relation to the plan can be outlined as follows

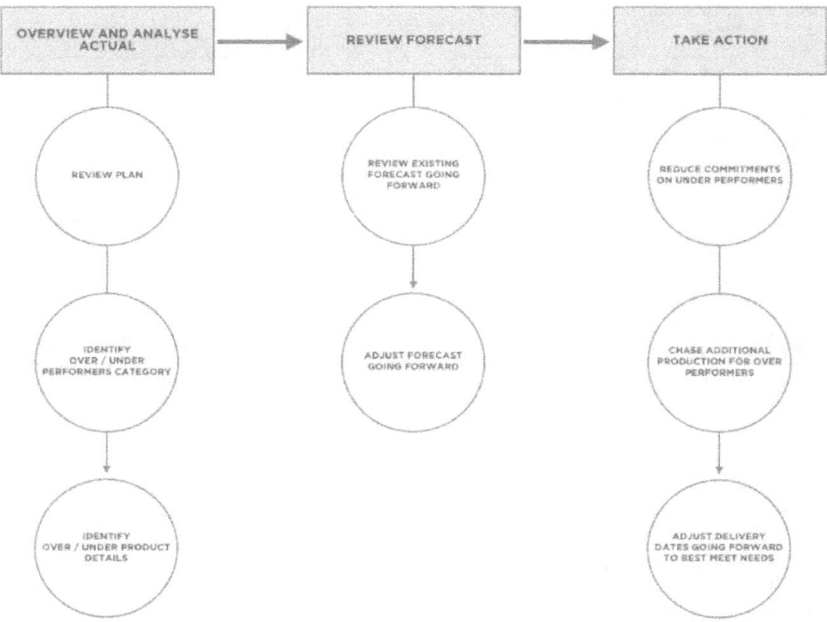

The start point of analysing and comparing the actual performance to the intended plan at a point in time, is to firstly to compare actual sales to date at total departmental level and drill down to product level and based on the result, review the planned sales for the balance of the season.

The potential new sales forecast is then compared to the actual commitment of product in the form of stock on hand at stores, product in transit and that at the supplier as well as the orders in the pipeline to determine the resultant shortage or surplus of stock.

The procedure which needs to be followed can be broken down into three distinct activities.

The recording of the total plan for the season in terms of sales and the planned breaking stocks at the end of the season as well as the current week's performance which has just been completed.

Based on the comparison of the actual sales to date in relation to that which was budgeted for may require a review of the balance of sales to be achieved and thereby create a revised forecast for the total season. The change in the sales forecast may also then require an adaptation of the planned breaking stocks to reflect the reality of the sales plan.

Once the realistic revised sales performance has been established, the result then needs to be compared to the total stock commitment and assessed whether there is sufficient stock in the pipeline to achieve the revised targets. If this is not the case, a plan has to be devised in order to determine what action is required to achieve this or conversely there may be a consequent surplus of stock which will have to be reduced.

Analysis options

Before deciding on what action is required there are consistent questions that need to be answered. In terms of why the sales differ to the plan one needs to determine whether the sales were early or late possibly due to seasonal factors or extraordinary events. However if they are low the question must be asked whether it is because the appeal to the customer is below expectation.

Measurement against key targets should also be considered as well as the guidelines that are outlined in the strategy. The proportions of the customer segmentation may be incorrectly projected. The pricing policy such as price tiering could be incorrectly balanced, new initiatives may be over optimistic or colour trends are not be as expected and therefore the deviation should be examined down to the lowest level of the hierarchy.

Key performance measures to focus on are forward cover targets to confirm that they are in line or if they are too low the reason may be that there is not enough stock in the system to enable achievement of targeted sales. The measures at store level need to be evaluated as the bigger selling stores may be significantly impacting sales if their individual targets are not being achieved.

It is key that all planned promotions and deliveries are still in line to be launched as scheduled and that there are no risks of late or non-delivery from the supplier as this will impact on performance for the balance of the season.

Historical comparison must be considered carefully especially in the case where events fall differently in that this year they may fall on the weekend instead of a week day as may have been the case in the previous year. Special events unique to the season could also have a significant effect. Much of this type of insight is gained through regular store and supplier visits, as well as strict adherence to meeting schedules that include all of the stakeholders comprising of buyers, merchandisers, allocators, designers and technologists. Working as a team keeps everyone involved and committed to an action plan complete with assignments and timelines and a system of updates that monitor the progress of action items.

Differing trends or patterns to that expected may have evolved such as prints which may emerge to be in higher demand than plains.

The review of better selling products as well as the worst sellers needs to be analytically done in an attempt to understand as to why they are performing as they are. Factors that may be common are styling features, colourations, functionality or fabrications. Styles programmed going forward should be reviewed for the identification of opportunities to adapt or change, move out or pull forward and if possible turn on or cancel production.

Regular probes on the sales floor and interaction with sales staff and customers often reveal obvious reasons which are commonly overlooked particularly when one is, as is typical, too close to the detail. Customer focus groups can also provide valuable comprehensions into the practical needs of the consumers and highlight opportunities where sales can be improved and poor quality issues may be exposed.

Sourcing strategy

Utilising the company, brand and buying group strategy together with the lifestyle and trend directions in conjunction with the research of prevailing market dynamics such as exchange rates, quotas and the local industry, a strategy as how to best source products will be drafted for the forward period which could be extended to cover the next few years.

The assessment of a prospective supplier or vendor, mill, dye house, fibre producer, processor, trimming and component contractor, packaging supplier and printer is a process that needs to be done thoroughly in order to ensure that they meet all the required criteria to manufacture the product in mind.

In principle there are four different methodologies of purchasing product.

The majority of garment purchases conducted by the retailer is based on inputs from the design, buying, merchandising and technical teams whereby the criteria of fabric, components, style and manufacturing as well as the packaging are dictated to the supplier in order for them to source from accredited suppliers.

Secondly, as is practiced by the more traditional retailers is where they buy their own fabric and allocate it out to a cut, make and trim supplier. The supplier may or may not offer a style, which could be provided by the retailer to a number of different suppliers to obtain a quote for the manufacture of the product according to a labour minute rating. The price of the fabric is static as it is supplied by the retailer. The downside of this methodology is that the retailer must have a technical understanding of fabrics which means that the buying team needs to be more knowledgeable and have added skills which are not always readily available in the labour market. There is also the need to invest in fabric stocks and have a detailed understanding of minute rates or manufacturing costs of the supplier. On the plus side of cut, make and trim manufacturing is that it enables the ability to cost accurately, be more flexible in selection of styling and achieve a greater speed to market.

A third methodology of sourcing is the direct purchase of a completed ready designed garment from the supplier where the retailer's brand label is inserted and the style is procured exclusively for the retailer.

Lastly there is the option to procure popular brands directly out of the supplier's range. In this case it is likely that there will be no flexibility in terms of modifying the style and often the investment of building a store within a store concept may be required. Pricing tends to be at a premium and commonly minimum order quantities apply.

The researching of new, cheaper, innovative and exciting sources of supply in order to maintain a competitive advantage in the market place is an ongoing process, as is the need to maintain a sustainable relationship with current core suppliers which comes with a continual effort to improve their delivery standards of product. Suppliers are expected to be consistently reliable, effective and efficient to retain the business of their clients as the success of the retailers is the guarantee of continued acceptance of the product that they produce.

A constant balance of those products which are sourced from local suppliers and that which are manufactured off shore is important. As off shore suppliers improve in terms of quality, equipment and workforce living standards there is an increasing pressure on costs and therefore the sources do not remain geographically static.

Fashion buying was originally focused in the Far East in Hong Kong and Taiwan but costs are increasing faster than they have in the past as well as pressure is being placed on authorities to elevate minimum wage bands. It is therefore not surprising that production is moving to more cost efficient areas such as Indonesia, Bangladesh, Pakistan, Cambodia, and Vietnam while production in Madagascar and Mauritius has also become prevalent.

Hong Kong and Taiwan have now become more the management and design centres who procure from alternative production plants. The ease of increased technology, the relaxing of bureaucratic barriers as well as cheaper travel has enabled the transfer of production to be relatively easy and flexible. Migration of production to newer countries brings limitations and therefore it is important to maximise efficiencies in the current countries where goods are produced while at the same time sourcing alternative manufacturing plants that will meet the ethical and quality standards of the retailer.

Added to this is the probability that the larger the offshore supplier is, the more the likelihood is that the retailer will be less important in their lives and if need be, the order can be more easily forfeited. The converse is that if the overseas supplier is small the possibility exists that the production may be outsourced to other vendors who the retailer may not even know about. Overseas factories seldom readily have excess production capacity and that this together with the longer transport lead times make the possibility of repeat orders within the same season improbable.

Sourcing internationally does, at face value, often appear to be very attractive but there are factors that need to be taken into account which can lead to additional unforeseen costs as well as logistical challenges particularly in terms of lead times. The re-organisation of production can therefore be perplexing and the savings that may be apparent up front could indeed be decimated later down the line.

Keeping track of the off shore supply chain at times presents some complex challenges and makes it very difficult to monitor the progress of product at all times. An extreme illustration of such a scenario is where the process commences with the raw material producer who passes the product onto the commodities traders whose purchasing agents sells them onto the garment manufacturers. In the procedure local distributors could be involved to deliver the raw materials to the garment manufacturing plant. Secondary vendors for outsourced processes are frequently utilised before the product is delivered eventually to the local exporters and freighters administered by agents on behalf of the larger trading houses who are the frontline liaison with the retailer.

Advantages may be enjoyed by having a dedicated foreign office in key cities to control the management of suppliers and product. Obviously this does come at an added cost and should only be considered when a critical mass in that foreign country is achieved. However, the formation of such an organisation must be assessed on merit as to whether it is viable or not. Typically such a team will consist of two or three merchandisers, possibly buying and sourcing specialists together with maybe three or four quality controllers who spend two to three days a week in the factories focusing exclusively on the retailer's orders. The foreign office owns the relationship with the supplier and are able to exert pressure to ensure critical deadlines are met. Communication is easier and faster as such teams are self-managed and can be flexible in evaluating priorities.

The extreme example of the complexity of dealing with offshore suppliers is that of the world's largest trading house being the Hong Kong based sourcing and logistical company, Li Fung. They own no factories or mills but simply play matchmaker between poor countries factories and vendors which have favourable labour rates and costs and the global retailers for whom Li Fung handle the logistics.

Li Fung represent some fifteen thousand suppliers across sixty countries which enable them to procure very high volumes and have them produced in a fraction of a time that a single supplier would take to complete. It is not surprising that consequently they are known as the "Walmart of purchasing" and the sheer size of the organisation makes it difficult to pin point the true sources of the product and they have been alleged from time to time to be linked to several calamities in some dubious factories.

Where the retailer is dominant in their target market and the volumes are substantial enough it is advantageous for them to cut out the middleman agent and procure directly from the source. By doing this an advantage is gained over their competitors and they do not end up subsidising the supply chain for their rivals especially where full containers are bought on a repeat basis. Advantage is also to be gained through using a buying agent or consolidator to combine the products into full container loads where they purchase from multiple off shore suppliers.

Currency exchange rate fluctuations may well change the advantage of buying off shore, as will quota limitations which could change in the exporting country due to the fact that costs will probably increase should the availability of the quotas become scarcer.

The management of offshore deliveries is more complex and if minimum order quantities are imposed they can lead to higher storage costs and inventory investment together with varying transport charges.

The intricate nature of international freight forwarding requires either an in house dedicated team or the need to outsource this function to an agency to take on the responsibility.

Often the additional travelling and increased management costs are not taken into account when considering product quotations. The opening of foreign offices with sourcing, quality control and buying teams in itself can be a considerable additional overhead that needs to be established, staffed and equipped and is excluded from the base garment cost.

Frequently the bulk offshore deliveries have to be unpacked and repacked and labelled after allocation that results in multiple handling which adds considerable cost and time delay.

For the reasons above the viability of sourcing from foreign suppliers has to be carefully considered in terms of the minimum volumes that need to be procured to achieve the benefits while at the same time being able to exceed the sales potential without putting strain on the warehouse storage capabilities.

It is therefore strategically beneficial if the supply chain from overseas is as short as possible with the minimum of cross over proprietorship points, for example, the allocation of product while it is in transit lessens the pressure of receiving and warehousing of the goods before being withdrawn for picking and packing. The possibility exists that the goods can bypass the storage stage and be delivered directly to the pick pack areas of the distribution centre. This type of approach might be appropriate for one off promotions and special events.

The advantages of a local supplier base is quicker potential delivery to market, more flexible production with easily manageable inventory quantities and less complicated administration, quality control and payment methodologies. For local suppliers the trend has also shifted towards smaller production infrastructures with specialisation on exclusivity and individualistic styling.

The relationship between retailers and local suppliers is most often one of mutual interdependence all of which has to be weighed up against the cost and innovation advantages of off shore suppliers. The manufacture of replenishment core type product is better suited to local manufacturers as it calls for the fine-tuning of styles, colour and size ratios which are easier to adjust. There may also be pressure from the authorities to encourage local production through the various "Buy Local" promotions in order to stimulate the local industry and satisfy the employment initiatives in the political arena.

It stands to reason that the less suppliers there are, the less the burden of supplier management will be with regard to different administration models, quality control and varying costs.

A strategy to rationalise suppliers eliminates smaller, incompatible, problematic suppliers who are often more demanding in terms of the time required to manage them compared to the effort spent on more substantial, streamlined producers and enable effective performance management.

The larger the quantities allocated to fewer suppliers will lead to lower cost prices through the economies of scale advantage as well as the benefit of the delivery of improved quality and reliability. Management communication and the mutual interdependence with specialised service provision will undoubtedly lead to a competitive advantage.

There are however risks involved in dealing with too few suppliers in that the exposure to greater innovation is limited and complacent suppliers tend to offer more and more of the same or wait for the retailer to provide ideas and designs. Often the production methods are inflexible which could result in a relationship of mistrust and frustration.

Newer suppliers can be added to the core base of suppliers, however, the number of suppliers in total should remain constant through the consistent measurement of performance including formal review processes being in place for existing suppliers. If they do not meet the performance criteria they run the risk of elimination.

The performance review and assessment of suppliers should not be done in isolation by each department that they supply but preferably conducted across the business as a whole which will deliver more objective and consistent results and thereby will avoid mixed messages being given to suppliers.

Other pitfalls that retailers need to be aware of is the differing perceptions of the suppliers versus that of the buyers. Typically buyers view suppliers as being frequently older and more experienced, full of excuses and promise the world. From the suppliers point of view the buyers are young and inexperienced, abuse their buying power and utilise threats to make unrealistic demands and apart from being busy all the time, the formation of a sustainable relationship is disrupted due to the regular changing of staffing in departments.

It is not uncommon that buyers and designers tend to make last minute changes to designs, trims, quantities and colours which puts immense pressure on suppliers and consequently leads to the need to work excessive overtime hours or over book production capacity. As a result they may end up using unqualified outside vendors in an effort to accommodate the revised unreasonable deadlines and can thereby easily transgress the compliance criteria.

Conscious efforts are essential to influence the relationship to be one of joint co-operation and respect, the conducting of informed cost price negotiations with better transparency with regard to each other's needs and the working together to achieve solutions that will be for their mutual benefit.

There are some key questions that need to be answered before embarking on a relationship with a potential supplier which are:

What are the supplier's capabilities and specific skills?

Do they have design facilities and what level of innovation is evident?

Do they have the capacity requirements to meet the required volumes?

Is the planning of production stable in that it minimises changeovers and keeps labour fully utilised so that orders are not shifted around dependent on which customer is shouting the loudest.

Are they financially stable? Do they meet the criteria that ensures payment to their raw material suppliers being secure and guaranteed?

Do they have the appropriate equipment to deliver the envisioned product?

Is the production sub contracted to other vendors and do these producers also meet the same required compliance standards?

What are the initial costing indications in comparison to alternative sources?

Which other major retailers do they supply?

What management and liaison structures are in place?

What are their quality standards like and do they have current valid compliance audits from an accredited recognised test house?

Do they have the ability to produce or source in smaller batches to maximise flexibility and speed?

How close are they to their component suppliers?

Where are they located and will that have any bearing on meeting the delivery lead times, delivery demand schedules and costs?

Do they have any long term strategic expansion plans?

Does the physical building structure meet all building specifications, safety requirements and provide the appropriate facilities to accommodate a production environment?

Is there evidence that they are ethically compliant in terms of staff hours of work, remuneration policies and adherence to accepted norms of terms of employment?

Do they meet the environmental requirements in terms of health and safety of the workers?

Do they utilise any banned substances in the production process and what is the policy for the safe disposal of waste effluent?

Are the raw material suppliers reputable and certified?

What are their laboratory facilities or which testing facilities do they use?

The format of these initial audits can be formalized in a matrix form and scorecard values can be weighted according to the level of importance that can be depicted through a relative score compared to other suppliers which ensures a more objective assessment and structured plans of action for suppler selection.

A simple example of such a supplier rating matrix is as follows

	QUALITY	CAPACITY	GROWTH	COSTING	ENVIRON-MENT	SOCIAL	INNO-VATION	LIAISON	TOT	WEIGHTED AVERAGE
WEIGHTED IMPORTANCE	6	6	5	7	5	5	5	6		
SUPPLIER A	20	15	25	30	15	15	10	20	150	108
SUPPLIER B	25	20	30	25	20	20	25	10	175	123
SUPPLIER C	30	30	10	25	20	20	30	20	185	132

Key areas of compliance focus in the drafting of an audit report

Social compliance refers in the main as to how the company treats its employees and their perspective on social responsibility. The point of reference is to a minimal code of conduct that directs how employees are treated with regards to wages, working hours, work conditions, safety signage and preventative measures such as lighting, electrical wiring and use of face masks, recruitment criteria, human resource policies in terms of disputes and promotions. What is absolutely essential is that they adhere to a set code of ethics to meet the compliance requirements.

Environmental compliance speaks to the respect that they have for environmental aspects such as the use of chemicals that may harm employees, disposal of waste products, pollution of water sources and the utilisation of environmental enhancing components such as the use of organic cottons. Compliance audits ensure that they meet the minimum standards of various environmental laws.

Supplier capabilities refers to the standards of vendors and their sources such as mills, trimming manufacturers, distributors and other collaborators in the supply chain who are audited and assessed. They need to provide vital management control for process safety, security and risk management. Audits focus on the policies and procedures to verify compliance with regulatory requirements and industry standards. The programmes must be properly designed and implemented as well as identify deficiencies and recommendations can be made as to where corrective actions may be required.

Audits are done by stages, the first being the gathering of information through visual observation, documented reviews and interviews with staff. This data is then compared to the regulatory requirements and an evaluation is made as to how they conform to the legal stipulations which forms part of the pre audit. The second phase of the audit would be an intense on-site inspection which includes the conducting of interviews and review of records to assess the effectiveness of the implementation of programmes. Lastly the post audit consists of the briefing of management on the findings and the preperation of a final report and the relevant rating with corrective action recommendations.

Such audits should be conducted on an annual basis by a recognized audit company such as SMETA, WRAP or SA 8000. This should be followed up by physical visits to the plants. Audits are not limited to the point of manufacture but ought to also include the raw material sources, processing houses or any other out sourced functions at other vendors.

It is important that such reports are kept on record and up to date as in the event of a disaster such as a fire, building collapse or accident they will serve as critical points of reference.

Supplier introduction

Prior to commencing business with a new supplier it is required that the retailer briefs the supplier on all aspects of conducting business with them. This will apply to all processes that are in place to get them up and running and what is needed to be adhered to in order to maintain healthy relations thereafter.

The type of information that should be provided to the supplier is the background of the retail company and the philosophies as well as the type of operations in place so that they have a high level understanding of the company values that are subscribed to.

The supplier needs to have a crystal clear understanding of the end to end process which must be followed to become a certified supplier. This process will include the complete account registration, bank details and references, contractual agreements, settlement of payment terms and conditions and subscription to any software programmes that may be required to conduct business.

All conditions and guidelines in doing business should be outlined in a manual so that there is a detailed point of reference in the event of any dispute that may arise. Often the manual and other relevant information is available on the retailer's website for easy reference as is any training material together with ongoing updates and communications. The site may be access controlled even to the point that the information available is specific to the supplier. An example of such information is where the supplier is able to monitor the sales performance of their product in real time. It is essential that the channels of communication are structured and very clear as poor exchange of information has a negative impact and causes additional cost through wasted time, effort and resources which could result in late deliveries which will undoubtedly reflect in the end as lost sales.

Processes should be outlined for support and training usually in the form of instruction guides or is done practically in a lecture room environment. Representative topics would be for example, best practices for picking and packing, processing of orders and reporting availability of product. More technical training could be the procedures for the use of specific software packages, analysis and use of management reports or the use of a product critical management tool.Performance management reports of the supplier should also be available in order that any shortcomings may be addressed promptly and enable the supplier to improve the efficiency of their operation. The type of key performance indicators that are measured, reported on and tolerances set are the analysis of customer returns, the measurement of actual variances to ordered quantities, the accuracy of picking and packing of product as well as the lead times of deliveries between receipt of orders and delivery to the retailer's receiving point.

A vital point to be measured is the rate of attrition during the production process which is the loss of product through rejects, under production through short delivery of raw materials or pilferage in the factory which results in loss of sales and needs to be analysed to keep these pre delivery instances to a minimum.

Customer returns must not only be quantified but the nature of the complaints have to be categorised and thresholds set to determine when a bulk return to supplier is warranted. The real danger lies where it is essential to retain the brand integrity when the nature of the defect can be considered dangerous or maybe life threatening and requires urgent withdrawal of the product from all points in the supply chain as well as the need to communicate a recall of the affected product through the media.

Where tolerances are set and the agreed criteria are not met, a consequence of some form or other may well be applied which usually has a financial implication through penalty discounts being enforced, rejection of delivery and the implementation of sale or return agreements.

Supplier manuals

The topics and information which is usually covered in the manual that may well form part of the memorandum of agreement are as follows

- The process that has to be followed to set up an account and the registration of the administrative details such as contact details, payment terms and logistical addresses. Retailer contact and help desk information is also published.
- Where the retailer may have unique software programmes for the conducting business such as the processing of orders, reporting of stock availability, the transfer of delivery instructions and product critical path management may require the supplier to invest in the packages and if need be upgrade the hardware to meet specifications to run such packages.

- All details of systems and reports generated should be described in sufficient detail to allow the supplier to be able to refer to in order to resolve any queries they may have.
- The manual must outline technical guidelines and testing requirements as well as packaging specifications and approved suppliers should be listed.
- Invoicing methods and the information that needs to be appear on such documents as well as the payment channels and methods have to be described in detail.
- Ticketing details, ticket examples, reference numbers and order process should appear together with a list of approved ticket printing houses as well as the consequences which are in place should goods be delivered without or with incorrect ticketing.
- Packaging specifications should be itemised with regard to outer cartons, pack quantities, sealing guidelines, weight tolerances and markings which have to appear on the cartons.
- The guidelines and processes that need to be followed to complete the delivery of product to the retailer's receiving point in terms of equipment handling, time slot booking, descriptive labelling and the like must be described in detail.
- The shipping documents utilised and the information that is required for off shore need to be noted as well as any specific administration processes that have to be followed.
- A detailed description is included of performance indicators and tolerances that are measured.
- The penalty levels which are applied where performance criteria are not met should be clearly stated in the manual as well as the methodology of the calculation to avoid disputes if and when the occasion arises.

Typical contractual contraventions are where the supplier's quality is found to be substandard and to be eligible for penalisation. Examples are quality failures in production, in cases where the safety of the product is compromised in the form of needle points or staples being found in the product, the use of poor attachments which carry the danger creating sharp edges on the garment that may pose a hazard to the consumer and the subcontracting of production to unauthorised vendors.

Clear guidelines and procedures as to the disposal of product need to be stated in the instances of the total withdrawal of product, production overruns, rejects and after what time period and which labelling or ticketing must be removed. Options that exist will be agreed on by the two parties for settlement of claims, for example, it may not be viable to incur reverse logistical costs to return distressed goods back to offshore suppliers and would be better to dispose of them locally. The recovery value would then be part of the settlement agreement with the supplier.

Protection of the retailer's intellectual property must be made very clear to all suppliers and this will pertain in the main to the safety of patents such as those relating to invention, utility or design. Trademarks are unique names, phrases, logos, symbols and can include colours which appear on the products themselves that are undoubtedly associated with the brand.

In the same way that the focus of the manual is on how to do things, the other side of the coin which is as important is the procedures to follow in order to exit from a supplier for whatever reason. It is not simply a case of no longer issuing orders and ceasing contact as there are certain processes which need to be clearly followed and signed off. These will include the deregistration of the account, the removal from all communication channels such as email distribution lists, elimination from access to any sensitive information on company websites and formal notification to all interested parties such as logistics, technology, marketing and financial departments.

Style briefing

Initially the supplier will be briefed conceptually as to what the product entails. The key information that is communicated is typically a sketch, photo, CAD print or sample with details. The detail will indicate design features, entail fabric and finish qualities, measurement guidelines, size range and ratios, colour ways, pricing and number of deliveries.

It is important that the supplier is provided with as much information as possible that is easily understood by even the most junior staff of the supplier especially in cases where English is not the first language. A principle of over communication and simplification should be followed to ensure complete clarity.

Meetings need to be handled professionally and follow a well prepared agenda and response to any queries have to be concise, well communicated and understanding needs to be tested. Detailed minutes and action plans with time scales attached should be clearly documented. Apart from the formal meetings, ongoing communications can be conducted via Skype and e-mail threads or conference calls.

Other information that can be included on a product specification document apart from the general information above is that pertaining to the inner packing, inserts and labelling. The product packaging minimum requirements and the methodology of the packing must be of a quality to withstand the rigours of transport, varying temperatures, inter warehouse transporting and mechanical handling.

A simple example of a style briefing sheet would look as follows

STYLE BRIEF		DATE	1 March
DEPARTMENT	Ladies T-Shirts	SUPPLIER	ABC
REFERENCE NUMBER	12345678	MNFR NUMBER	44455
DESCRIPTION	Ladies T-Shirt	SILHOUETTE	Top
DELIVERY DATE	20 September	NECKLINE	Round
UNITS	1,000	SLEEVE	Short
SIZES	Small 20% Medium 50% Large 30%	FIT	Regular
COLOURS	White 40% Beige 30% Red 30%	PRICE	129.00
FABRIC / YARN	100% Cotton Single Jersey Quality 12345	PHOTO / SKETCH	
STYLE COMMENTS	Piping must be contrast white.		

Specification pack

The product specification pack is the detailed briefing document used to clearly communicate the product details to the buying, design and technical teams as well as suppliers.

Components of the product specification pack

COMPLETION DATES

PATTERNS / MEASUREMENTS

SKETCH PHOTOS

LABELLING AND PACKING

FABRIC AND TRIMS

WASH CARE DETAILS

PRODUCT SPECIFICATION PACK

ATTRIBUTE OPTIONS

BILL OF MATERIAL DETAIL

PRICE DETAILS

ASSORTMENT DETAILS

SIZE RANGE

TECHNICAL TESTS

The type of information that should be included is

A sketch or digital picture, the season, the product name and reference number, fabric technical information, fit specifications, size details, quantities, sample sizes, delivery dates, packaging and placement of ticketing, outer packaging requirements, display materials such as hanger reference number, folding guidelines, details of required stitches and seams, trim card and placement details, garment sewing instructions, etc.,

This will enable the supplier to produce a first sample and provide a detailed quote of cost price.

The technologist will be responsible to provide the bill of materials, the test requirements for the fabric, trim and product, any finishes that are required, safety requirements, fit and block stipulations, wash care instructions as well as provide an assessment of the supplier capabilities to produce the product.

Supplier meetings

Once the product specification pack is formulated for a particular style, the retailer is in a position to initiate detailed meetings in order to prepare the supplier prior to the commencement of the production process.

It is extremely important that the meetings are well structured, prepared with an agenda, are clear and professional. Most importantly it is critical that the appropriate people are assigned tasks and completion dates are recorded for follow up.

Live information capture using a laptop and projector is very effective as meetings tend to be shorter, decisions and assignments are clear and results can be managed and tracked. The other advantage is that the publication of the minutes is immediate with the action tasks for those accountable being explicitly defined with completion dates.

Negotiating

Negotiation is the process whereby through dialogue between two or more parties an agreement is met and the outcome satisfies the needs of both within the boundaries that the situation will allow.

In the retail environment, negotiations typically revolve around topics such as price, garment content, costs, innovation and profitability. The discussions can take place under high pressure where the expectations of both parties are elevated and the rivalry is intense. Often the relationship may be under threat which may or may not add another dimension depending how significant the association is. The opposite of this can be, and the most suitable, where the two parties collaborate to reach the most desired outcome.

To achieve a situation where both parties benefit, requires maturity, a clear understanding of the end objectives with informed discussions by both parties and the development of a plan to achieve a mutual objective.

Notwithstanding the above the supplier and the retailer will still have their own agendas. The supplier will wish to sell as much as he can for the best price while the retailer will want the product for as cheap as possible for the best quality. If the retailer does not have an insightful understanding of the manufacturing process the chances are that they might end up paying too much or sacrificing content.

Negotiating can be a traumatic experience and not all may have the appetite for the heightened discussion. In the case of the supplier there could be a tendency to avoid the confrontation and at times simply give the product to the retailer for the price requested, while the retailer, on the other hand, will similarly pay the supplier's more expensive proposal without exploring all options to get the best deal.

The retailer must always be well prepared with all relevant facts regarding fabric, trim, ratings and costs, prevailing exchange rate trends, wage structures, margin policies including other external and internal factors at hand in order to be able to have an informed sincere discussion. The persuasion process must be done in a way that the argument is convincing and the acceptance by the other party is seen to be mutually beneficial, trustworthy and incorporates the other participant's needs.

The progression of negotiation follows the steps of preparation, conducting the discussion and reviewing the outcomes.

Thorough preparation is critical which requires that the issues and opportunities are identified, prioritised and have a value for both parties. Focus must be on both the hard subjects such as the monetary issues and volumes as well as the softer matters such as perceptions.

Boundaries must be set in the types of outcome broken up into which would ideally like to be achieved, or what is likely to be achieved and thirdly the bare minimum that would be accepted.

Analysis of the environment of both businesses must be well defined in terms of the markets, competitor activities and the supplier capability and technical expertise required. These factors coupled to the trading history and what percentage the supplier is of the retailer's business and what the retailer represents of the supplier's total production or put differently, who needs who the most.

Past performance and consistency as well as the growth potential and the degree of product uniqueness or cost advantages are important leverage factors that are to be taken into consideration.

Key bargaining points for the retailer are cost prices, discounts, volumes, exclusivity, return policies, promotional support, delivery scheduling and any other unique service while the supplier's focus is likely to be the volumes that can be achieved, the highest cost price that will be agreed and the long term sustainability of regular business.

There is not always a satisfactory resolution to negotiation discussions and contingency plans need to be in place as to what alternatives are available should a deadlock situation be reached. These may include the possibility of moving production to different suppliers, reduce volumes and increasing the levels of other substitution ranges, the consideration of sale or return agreements and although not desirable, possibly increasing the selling price above the norm.

Behaviour and strategies during the meeting are extremely important. Asking for more than is expected will give room for negotiation to what is acceptable without simply accepting the first offer. It is also essential to remain flexible and creative in an effort to avoid a deadlock situation. A vital point to bear in mind is that at all costs to avoid haggling as this practice runs the risk of destroying a relationship.

If confrontation does transpire, it should be tactically done and at all costs does not include any personal attack or involve the use of threats and ultimatums. The power of silence should be remembered as it can be effective and if needs be, try and concede to small bits at a time, park potentially unresolvable issues even if it means that the meeting has to be temporarily adjourned.

There are personal factors that can influence the final negotiation. Different partakers follow different processes, they have diverse experience levels as well as possess varying understandings and personality traits which may be unpredictable.

There is an added complexity in dealing with off shore suppliers where there are duties, logistical challenges, and culture and language differences.

Once the negotiations are concluded, a documented summary of the agreements, commitment of resources, capacity to deliver and action plans is absolutely critical to ensure complete understanding. The record will enable an amicable resolution should any misinterpretation which could possibly become a point of dispute at a later stage.

Technical strategy

The technical teams need to sanction that the correct fabrics, components, dyestuffs and finishes are used and developed to meet the design and buying strategies and the goods are manufactured to the stated quality standards that are offered within the price structure policy.

As the focus is on the technical aspects of the products a careful balance needs to be established as to what the best match is between that which is technically acceptable compared to the commercial viabilities. In order to achieve the right balance there needs to be mature collaboration between the buying and technical teams.

Innovation and refined development opportunities are identified as part of the technical strategy and the plan of action and accountabilities are stipulated to achieve a competitive advantage and thereby improve market penetration.

Technical Teams consist broadly of the fabric and garment technologists. Fabric technologists are highly trained specialists who focus on typically woven or knitted disciplines. Specialised products such as knitwear, tailoring and footwear require added knowledge of components and specific production machinery.

A major portion of the fabric technologist's task is the development and innovation of new fabrics and the enhancement of existing products. New fibres and blends of fibres such as the blending of natural and synthetic fibres, addition of chemicals to finishing process will possibly lead to new inventions and improvements such as better washability, softer handles, easy care properties like easy to iron, crease resistant finishes, rot resistant applications, seamless or seams that are glued that allow for smoother looks particularly for under garments, the evolvement of elastane products such as lycra which revolutionised active and casual wear and the enhancement of thermal properties of winter undergarments. The success of such developments which add to the profitability as well as the form and function necessitates a close working relationship with suppliers, mills and value adders.

Garment technology have the responsibility to ensure that the make-up of the garment meets the set down criteria and the components like buttons, interlinings and threads are of the standard that is functional and are not inferior.

Many factories have developed specified technological capabilities that have been built around the production of a particular category of garments relevant to them which vary from factory to factory or even within the same plant. The garment technologist must understand this implicitly and exploit this knowledge to its fullest.

The relationship with the commercial team is sometimes strained as the ideal level of form and function can be challenged by the need to market the product at the most commercially competitive price.

The objective of the garment technologist is to ensure that quality is not compromised. The tasks essential to achieve this can be varied, for example, the assessment of potential manufacturers and fabric mills to ensure that the established standards are achievable, the specification of raw materials, overseeing sampling stages and ensuring that any delays which may result through the process do not compromise the delivery prerequisites.

In safeguarding that the all quality standards are met particularly through the inspection of garments, inspectors need to possess specific skills. Quality controllers should be ethical, sincere and honest, open mindedly being willing to consider alternatives, be diplomatic and tactful in their dealings with people and are able to actively observe their surroundings as well as perceive and adapt to varying situations.

The technologist has an intimate knowledge of the supplier base through historical awareness as well as from continually researching new and existing suppliers. As the sourcing specialist they have to guide buying teams in the selection of the most appropriate manufacturer for the various types of product. It is also very essential that they are conscious of the fabric prominence for the forthcoming season as dictated by the strategies and budget levels to ensure that there is sufficient capacities at the relevant mills to meet the overall demands without compromising quality.

The task of assessing potentially new suppliers is a role that may be included in the stable of the technical team or it may be hived off to defined sourcing specialists who are knowledgeable team members that recognise the strengths and weaknesses of suppliers and based on this where best to place orders accordingly.

Suppliers are assessed on various criteria such as their management infrastructure, financial stability, specialised equipment availability, fabric specialty, levels of innovation, fashion or basic production orientation, the other retailers they serve, their flexibility of cost negotiability and social responsibility policies. Other external factors that may well influence the selection of suppliers could be those like prevailing exchange rates, remuneration policies and physical locality.

With the focus mainly on the planning and buying infrastructure required to procure product and ensure the efficiencies that will enable the maximization of the profit opportunities. However it has to be remembered this will not be achieved unless the product is as close to perfect in terms of meeting predetermined quality standards, the addition of new or innovative features, is safe and meets the ever changing social and global needs. These are the factors or pillars that underpin the very reason for the existence of technology.

Quality

A product achieves a high standard of quality if it presents well on display, fits well, wears well, washes well, is fit for purpose, offers value for money, is free from any defects, insufficiencies and is unhampered from deviance to standards.

The activities need to ensure that the product meets the stated design, technical tolerances, fit, and fabric and colour specifications. This is often easier said than done. Supplier capabilities must be freely available to achieve this as well as the fact that unclear communications of expectations and standards may result in specifications not being met due to time and cost pressures.

Innovation

In order that the offering remains competitive it is imperative that new features or attributes are implemented constantly. For this to happen it requires the continual investment in new, improved ways of developing and producing product or materials. Innovation may be related to the fabric, components, treatments, end product attributes, packaging or sources of supply.

Inventive construction can add value the garment in terms of form and function such as adjustable waistbands for improved comfort. The secure lock stitching of buttons and other small items on children's garments which reduce the possibility of them being swallowed. The use of especially engineered interlinings which have more resilience enable garments to be totally machine washable, for example in the case of men's suits.

Social and environmental responsibilities

In the modern day and age most people are very aware of the responsibilities that suppliers are required to meet in order to keep the world as sustainable as possible.

The use of organic fabrics like cotton that is derived from organically grown crops, the unsavoury practice of child labour in production process, the structures in place for the removal of chemical wastes and many others are issues which are continually challenged.

The evolution of production units in China initially did not see environmental awareness as a primary focus as they were more concerned with survival but as they have developed, the treatment of waste and use of electricity has become a more important factor to be considered and the laying down of guidelines and regulations have become the norm. Although the Chinese have become environmentally sensitive and implement environment protection measures there is still the tendency to focus more on the protection of personal health. The situation is in the process of slowly improving to protect other environmental factors largely due to the improved education standards of younger management.

The key points of attention for sustainable environment awareness is the measurement and constantly improving efforts to reduce electricity consumption with the reduction of energy targets in place and the use of solar panel technology or even something as simple as the siting of administration desks next to windows. The same applies to the reduced use of water and where possible the practice to use recycled water has been introduced.

Safety

The safety of the customer must always be paramount as there are volumes of examples of where people have been injured or worse due to unsafe or defective product. Technology should constantly strive to meet the highest standards of safety in their products as well as that of the plants in which they are manufactured and the logistical process that is followed in order to get the product to market. Where required, the customer should be fully informed of particular risks inherent to the products.

If supplier's products do not conform to safety regulations they are subject to risks particularly where the required certificates are not available to show that they have met the obligatory regulations. The standards should be documented on laboratory test reports and supported by the pre-production samples either completed by the retailer's technologists or an accredited independent third party external laboratory. In some of the large trusted suppliers there may be internal specialists who self-regulate this process but this may present a challenge where there is a broad range of product categories being manufactured.

Fabric Technology

In the buying arena an integral part of the role is a pre requisite knowledge of textiles and the beginning to end production process associated with garment creation. With a good understanding of fabrics the product appeal, value and innovation aspects can be maximised and the most appropriate material can be identified for a product that will deliver the required performance to best meet the end user requirements and expectations. The briefing and negotiating process with suppliers is also able to be conducted with greater authority and credibility.

Ongoing development of new fabrics is reliant on inputs from various sources such as that of designers, buyers, suppliers, mills, yarn providers as well as the dyestuff and chemical suppliers. A healthy interaction between the main players permit the fabric innovation decisions to be made earlier and consequentially enable quicker product development.

The production process using fibres converted to yarns together with processing through to the finished product can be outlined as follows

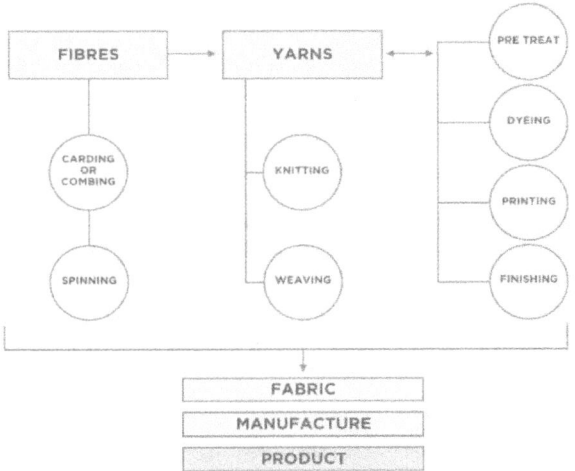

Fibres

The essential requirements for fibres to be spun into yarns is that it must be at least five millimetres in length and should be flexible and strong enough. Other inherent properties should include elasticity, durability and a measure of lustre.

Fibres are either natural which tend to be predisposed to irregularities or synthetic that are more consistent and easier to control. Through the blending of both types in varying proportions it is possible to achieve a bit of the best of both worlds.

The continual developments of new and blends of fibres have transformed the performance of many fabrics particularly in terms of the form, function, safety and fashionability. Typical examples of this is the reduction of creasing and the evolvement of easy care properties.

Staple fibres which are of defined lengths are used for the construction of both natural and synthetic yarns whereas man-made filament fibres are extruded from natural gases and oil and stretched into continuous strands to manufacture synthetic yarns.

The properties of fibres vary dependent on the source. Natural fibres such as cotton absorb moisture well but need to be well prepared to counteract shrinkage, stretching, fading or being eaten by fish moths. Synthetic polyester has good easy to care properties, does not shrink or stretch and is economical but is not very absorbent. A blended combination of yarns from natural and synthetic parents take on the characteristics of both and the extent to which this is achieved is dependent on the combined proportions.

Yarns

Yarn is a continuous length of twisted or interlocked fibres which are used in the production of textiles, crocheting, knitting, weaving, embroidery, and rope making. There are two types being staple yarns that are spun from natural fibres and filament yarns which are derived from synthetic fibres.

Spinning of yarns may be of the same fibre or can be a blend of natural and synthetic fibres in varying proportions. The properties of warmth, lightness, durability or softness of handle can be achieved to a higher or lesser degree through the varying of the ratios in the blending in order to best utilise the positive characteristics of each fibre. An example is the polyester and cotton blend where the original cotton characteristics of softness and breathability are retained whilst the polyester offers the strength, wrinkle and mildew resistance.

Cotton yarns can either be combed whereby during the process a stronger and more luxurious yarn is created and the hairy surplus of the fibre is removed in comparison to carded yarns which have less body and are more hairy.

Selling strategy

How the product is transferred into the customer's hands is largely dependent on the store format but the manner by which this happens can differ greatly.

In a typical supermarket and mass retail "stack 'em high" environment, transfer takes place whereby the customers serve themselves and payment is made at a checkout. In terms of self-service assistance the only interaction is through the request for help from a roving store staff member or shelf talkers.

The extreme opposite to this is where there is counter service and the customer is served by a dedicated staff member standing behind a unit which is more common in a specialist outlet such as a jewelry store or cosmetic counter.

The approach to the staffing of stores and the change of the roles from real people to technological options are becoming important considerations in the strategic development with regards to selling the product.

A common trend is to house signature ranges within large stores by creating a shop within a shop environment. The examples where this may be a bit indistinct is whereby the product is displayed on self-service shelves but the assistant to customer ratio is very high. An illustration of this is that of dedicated high fashion stores where specialised knowledge is required to assist the customer to make a considered decision. It is therefore absolutely essential to select the most suitable selling strategy option that will optimally serve the customer.

In the modern era of technology the internet is probably the fastest growing medium through which to sell product. Online websites now exist for all types of goods and all the major traders as well as dedicated online retailers are spending large amounts of money to set up their sites in such a way that they are very user friendly, faster and most attractive with secure, easy payment methods.

The main objectives of such sites is to enable the offer of products, create a level of trust and inspire the customer to make a purchase. The establishment of trust can be aided by the use of testimonials whereby the experience of past customers affirm the selling proposition.

Door to door deliveries at an additional fee or which alternatively may be absorbed by the retailer are carried out by sophisticated courier services from various highly efficient distribution centres. International purchases in foreign currencies are also relatively easy to do in this way and customers receive the parcels within a reasonable period of time.

Another option is that the retailer may choose to carry out picking of stock from brick and mortar stores which are in close proximity to the online customer but it should be noted that this choice does bring challenges in sustaining consistent full availabilities and maintaining accurate data integrity. Similarly, some retailers offer the facility of "click and collect" whereby the customer places an order on line and at a time convenient to them collects the order from a designated store.

The problem that customers do have is that they are not able to try on the garments so retailers need to devise some convenient special service options such as the provision of critical body measurements to assist in the determination of an appropriate size.

Marketing teams utilise various types of techniques to effectively expose the product in the most attractive way to the market. Traditional channels in the form of print, radio, television, in house magazines, flyers, and point of sale material as well as the use of innovative medium such as permeating fragrances and suitable background music or a store branded radio station all attempt to enhance the shopping experience. The use of posters and bill boards, scratch cards and the like are still very prominent in varying formats, however in increasing magnitudes, the creative use of the electronic channels by way of websites, sms, e-mail and social media such as facebook and twitter are now very evident.

The systematic collection of customer data through the interactive media allows the customer profiles to be analysed and targeted in a more scientific way. Loyalty programmes are very popular and mostly reward the customer either in the form of points which can be cashed in at a later stage for the purchase or provide an immediate discount at the till point. Such programmes are not only extremely effective in significantly improving sales and profits but they also allow the retailer to interpret in detail the buying habits of the customer and consequently thereby are able to better service the consumer needs.

While shopping generally refers to the activity of simply buying a product it has become very much a recreational activity whereby a visit to the shopping mall becomes a wonderful experience which may or may not necessarily result in any purchase being made. Some malls may have added attractions such as theatres, ice skating rinks, stages for entertainment and even larger magnetisms such as aquariums and fun parks while facilities such as gyms are not an uncommon appendage. Restaurant and fast food eateries are an integral part which are often positioned in centrally located food halls where both the major brands and specialised restaurants are represented.

The dominant tenants are the major retailers who are regarded to be the crowd pullers. The main mix comprise of large food chains together with typical mass clothing retailers while other stores such as general chains provide the bulk of hard and specialist goods like electronics, appliances, stationery, furnishings, jewelry, pharmaceuticals and sports shops.

A complex combination of line shops who derive their name due to the fact that they flank the interlinking walkways between the major tenants and tend to be more exclusive in their offerings. The rentals are usually at a much higher rate and the closest adjacency to a major tenant comes at a premium. Line shops will typically include outlets such as hairdressers, opticians, beauticians, boutiques, dedicated outdoor gear retailers, accessory specialists, luggage shops, photographic stores, religious retailers selling inspirational product and even tattoo parlours. Other options include the barrow type outlets selling product such as ties and accessories and specialized delicacies.

What is also evolving to a greater degree is the presence of international chains and brands from all over the world as it has become increasingly easy for stores to open due to improved technologies and exposure both from an IT perspective as well as the use of efficient transport methodologies. It has reached a stage where very few major retailers ignore opportunities to trade internationally especially where domestic markets have become saturated and increasingly competitive. The lure of new emerging markets are great but can be challenging in terms of the differing profiles of customers and culture considerations as well as the unforeseen detection of hidden costs.

Malls are strategically positioned close to residential dense areas and the science of the mix of line shops supported by the major tenants are largely influenced by the demographics of the area that they serve. Such malls may be supported by adjacent discount shopping centres which mostly include many clothing, shoe and factory outlet stores. Factory shops enable manufacturers or traders to market over runs, rejects, problem lines at reduced prices in locations that enjoy lower rentals. Liquor outlets, hardware stores and nurseries are also frequently seen adjacent to the main shopping complex.

A factor that should be addressed in the layout of malls is the ease of shopping and the implementation of plans for the free flow of traffic which does not stress the customers particularly during peak times when the mall corridors are jam packed with people. This state of affairs is leading to an ever increasing trend towards convenience shopping where the establishment of smaller shopping centres on the fringes of suburbs dispenses with the anxiety and lessens the time required to complete the shop.

The mall has largely been the cause of the demise of the "high street" store as is evident by the many major chain stores who have succumbed. The operations have consequently closed or have relocated to the shopping centres outside the city. However, there is still a place in certain instances for these stores to remain as is seen in some cities where there is in fact a reverse trend as there is still a density of office workers as well a growing inclination to live within the city centre which has led to surplus office space being transformed into apartment blocks or new developments being constructed.

Traditional general stores and co-operatives offering a broad range of everything for the community and mom and pop family run shops who purchased from the travelling salesman most commonly found in the rural areas are now very far and few between. Centralized shopping locations with all the relevant chains being represented including the influx of the discount shops specialising in goods from the East, some of which have originated from dubious sources, are now in almost every town. This has sadly relegated these old fashioned stores to no longer being in existence.

Franchise stores offer the opportunity for individual traders to invest in a mass retail group and enjoy the benefit of the support from the chain's branding, quality products and marketing strategies. The advantage for the franchisee is that the expansion and market penetration can be accelerated with external investment and they enjoy a commission for goods sold without the risk of stock holding costs, overheads and staffing expenses. The success of a franchise venture will depend mostly on enough working capital, reliable support from the franchisor and the emotional involvement in the business of the franchisee with suitable staff in the right location at affordable rentals.

In days gone by the goods were stored in walk-in counters often being displayed behind glass and in drawers with sales assistants serving the customer from within the unit as well as manning a till stationed at each counter. While this way of serving customers was very effective from an interaction point of view it soon became unsustainable due to the demands of mass retailing and convenience for the customer.

The newer formats of stores are well lit, uncluttered and appealing to the customer. They house easy to access product which is in sufficient quantities with well demarcated information through attractive signage. Displays whether on shelves, tables or garment rails are well thought out and coordinated in cameo presentations that are lit in such a way that suggest to the customer how the product pieces can be worn together in terms of lifestyle and colouration. Displays are adjacent to complementary customer needs, for example women's skirts will be located close to the blouse displays which will be adjacent to the ladies trousers. The ladies outerwear will most likely be next to the lingerie department which will lead into ladies sleepwear. There can also be a thread of the chosen similar colour themes throughout which are being promoted at that point in time.

Focus cameo displays as created by specialist visual merchandisers are located in highly visible areas such as aisles, window displays or walls which change regularly to convey the message of prevailing stories in order to attract and engage the customer. Seasonal changes, special events, promotional activity and colour themes are typically introduced in this way and thereby sustain the impact of newness, freshness and excitement. The customer not only has a pleasant experience considering the proposition but the potential opportunity of a sale is maximised.

Pay points and change rooms are conveniently placed and the design of these units are such that they lessen the frustration that comes with the inevitable waiting periods.

Personal interaction with the customer by any staff member whether they are the sales assistants or management can never be substituted. Service remains of paramount importance in ensuring that they can illustrate to the customer the ways in which styles and colours of the different components can tastefully be worn together.

The need for refurbishment and revitalisation of stores and displays is an ongoing process, which although being costly, regularly presents the customer with a fresh and exciting environment to enjoy the shopping experience and avoid being faced with stale, run down and drab looking stores that undermine even the most attractive merchandise.

Technology is fast changing the face of servicing the customer much in the same way the introduction of barcodes did in the past. The use of robots to replenish shelves as well as the counting of inventory or retrieval of orders is a reality in the making. Technical packages that measure the customer's preferential purchases and reconcile to previous purchases to feed the data base in order to understand and know the person are now common place. Other applications are such as the body metrics programmes that take body measurements in an instant and recommend the appropriate size of garments. At the checkout the process can be accelerated significantly where the trolley of product can be scanned as an entity without the comparative laborious task of handling, scanning and packing of the individual items. The viability of the investment and the impact on staffing structures in such like developments should be weighed up carefully against the competitiveness and efficiencies that they will deliver.

Supplier strategy

The relationships with suppliers is key to a successful business in order to ensure that the trade is sustainable and fair in the long term. The strategy needs to be formulated in a way that it safeguards the consistent achievement of the key performance targets, where there is regular feedback and a system of incentives and penalties can be applied to maximise the efficiencies. The strategy would stipulate that the relationship that should be strived for is to partner with suppliers who are dependable in terms of meeting delivery deadlines, supply the quantity requirements accurately, are cost efficient, maintain high quality standards, display innovation, have fair remuneration policies and are environmentally sensitive which will all be for the mutual benefit of both parties.

Supplier's performance and ranking needs to be evaluated, the margin policy and negotiation strategies such as open book costing, tenders or cross costing have to be reviewed to ensure that they are in line with the long term sourcing strategy.

Other components of the sourcing strategy will probably be the development of fast track manufacturers who will deliver product quickly to market at significant margins and outstanding value. With this will be possible rationalisation of number of suppliers allowing for simplicity and improved control according to a clear route map of planned supplier growth and decline.

Other processes required are the confirmation of core fabrics as well as the key mills. New potential suppliers, including packaging suppliers and countries have to be researched and identified.

Supplier manuals and starter packs must be updated where necessary including the key performance indicators by which the suppliers are measured and the resultant penalties or incentives have to be confirmed and communicated.

The risks that can be encountered are aggravated in certain situations such as with the movement of strategic product to new plants, or existing suppliers being utilised for different types of products which they may not adapt well to. The allocation of high volumes with a minimal quality assurance infrastructure in place as well the ability to meet critical launch dates require that performance measurement is critical for early identification of any potential failure.

A tough line has to be taken on dealing with substandard delivery and quality. Data collected from various sources needs to be accurate and reliable especially where a penalty system is applied for non-performance.

Customer returns have to be analysed and criteria put in place which may result in a penalty being applied for the number of returns in the form of a sliding scale. The analysis of the most common faults also highlights the areas of quality which need to be addressed.

The late or under completion of orders or non-conformance to size and colour ratios translate directly to lost sales and can be assessed and penalized either through a direct fine or a trade discount and possibly a sale or return arrangement. A word of caution with regard to a sale or return arrangement is although the goods that are not sold after a period of time can be returned, the sales of these goods may impact the performance of other similar products that are on offer at the same time which is not always taken into account.

Late deliveries measurement ensures that completion is on time according to the critical path. A typical example of a penalty is one which is on a sliding percentage scale of discount for every week that the delivery date is missed up to a pre-determined stage after which the order faces cancellation.

Lead times can be measured based on the time taken for the supplier to deliver to the retailer's back door. A realistic number of days can be set as a tolerance for the delivery of product based on mode of transport and distance from the retailer thereafter penalties may be activated. It does happen that the supplier may report the full availability of product but in reality part of the order may still be in production and the delivery may take place in the form of a number of split drops which would be unacceptable and is almost equivalent to fraud.

Order fill percentage represents what was actually delivered in comparison to what was ordered. Any deviation to this translates into lost sales from the lowest size level as the retailer is not receiving what was ordered.

The advantage of a controlled performance management system is the quick identification of poor performing suppliers. The more efficient suppliers welcome the performance measurements as it assists supplier management to more effectively manage their business, assign accountability and also be able to assess their contribution to sales performance and strive to benefit from the advantage of incentive schemes applied by the retailer where they exist.

It is preferable that such a reporting system is entrenched and is published on a monthly basis to the supplier and the internal buying groups. Such reports form a good basis of discussion in meetings with the supplier and alerts the buying team to potential problems that may be evolving. It should therefore be no surprise to the supplier if the need to apply penalties is necessary as sometimes the monetary value of the penalties could pose a major financial risk to a supplier.

Supplier performance management report

SUPPLIER ABC	RETAIL SALES		COST	SALES MARGIN	INTAKE RECEIPTS		INTAKE RECEIPTS MARGIN	CUSTOMER RETURNS		ORDER FILL RATE %	AVERAGE DAYS LEAD TIME
	Units	Sell value	Cost Value	% Margin	Units	Sell value	% Margin	Units	Returns % to Receipts	% Actual vs Order	No of days
JANUARY											
Group A	9800	250800	114616	54.3%	10000	252000	54.5%	9	0.09%	98%	4.6
Group B	14500	750650	333289	55.6%	16000	760700	56.2%	7	0.04%	87%	4.9
Group C	4800	610500	276557	54.7%	5000	630000	56.1%	19	0.38%	100%	5.1
Total	29100	1611950	724461	55.1%	31000	1642700	55.9%	35	0.11%	93%	4.7
FEBRUARY											
Group A	8900	170300	77997	54.2%	12000	172000	54.7%	1	0.01%	100%	4.1
Group B	16500	730900	320865	56.1%	18000	750000	57.2%	2	0.01%	85%	6.2
Group C	4800	550850	245679	55.4%	6000	555000	55.7%	5	0.08%	90%	4.8
Total	30200	1452050	644542	55.6%	36000	1477000	56.4%	8	0.02%	95%	5.3
MARCH											
Group A	7200	180700	90169	50.1%	9000	181000	50.2%	7	0.08%	58%	4.1
Group B	20800	900340	533902	40.7%	23000	910500	41.4%	6	0.03%	91%	5.2
Group C	7900	880750	453586	48.5%	10000	890200	49.0%	2	0.02%	92%	5.1
Total	35900	1961790	1077657	45.1%	42000	1981700	45.6%	15	0.04%	63%	4.8
AUTUMN											
Group A	25900	601800	282782.3	53.0%	31000	605000	53.3%	17	0.05%	87%	5.2
Group B	51800	2381890	1188055	50.1%	57000	2421200	50.9%	15	0.03%	93%	5.1
Group C	17500	2042100	975821.9	52.2%	21000	2075200	53.0%	26	0.12%	97%	4.2
Total	95200	5025790	2446659	51.3%	109000	5101400	52.0%	58	0.05%	90%	4.8

The performance report is for a specific supplier for a sub season January to March which will be autumn in the southern hemisphere or spring in the northern hemisphere. The values are reflected for each product group that the supplier manufactures for.

The retail sales in both units and selling value represent the sales through the till.

Cost is the value that the retailer paid the supplier for the goods.

The % margin is deduced from the sales value that was rung up on the till including any promotion or reduced goods in relation to the cost paid for the goods.

Intake receipts represent the units and selling value of product received from the supplier at the retailer's back door.

The % margin is therefore the contract selling value of the product relative to that what was paid for the goods.

The value of customer returns is reflected as the number of returns in relation to the amount of goods received expressed as a percentage. An acceptable percentage will be set as a tolerance and should this be exceeded a penalty system may well be applied.

The order fill rate reflects the percentage delivery of product at the lowest level, e.g. size compared to that what was ordered. If the delivery contravenes the agreed acceptable tolerance consequences may well be applied.

The average lead time is the number of days that it takes for the goods to leave the distribution point of the supplier and reach the back door of the retailer. If the time is greater than the number of days which is set as reasonable it may also attract a fine.

A penalty may be in the form of a financial fine or discount and in extreme cases could be a total cancellation of the contract. Agreements may alternatively be entered into whereby the delivery is accepted but should sales not take place prior to an agreed date the retailer will be entitled to return the goods.

Apart from the mathematical measures that are illustrated above, there are the qualitative measures that need to be evaluated when assessing the performance of a supplier. These categories would include factors such as commercial acumen, financial stability, value management and corporate continuity and governance.

From the planning perspective the production capacity availability and consistency of product supply is also an important factor coupled to robust quality assurance systems.

The level of design and innovation offering remains an important aspect that the supplier is judged on. Apart from technical compliance, social compliance and logistical complexity also plays a significant role.

A negotiation strategy should be utilised that delivers the greatest benefit and minimises cost whilst also reducing risk. In the retail environment, negotiations typically revolve around topics such as price, garment content, costs, innovation and profitability. The discussions can take place under high pressure where the expectations of both parties are elevated and the rivalry is intense. Often the relationship may be under threat which may or may not add another dimension depending how significant the association is. The opposite of this can be, and the most suitable, where the two parties collaborate to reach the most desired outcome. The retailer must always be well prepared with all relevant facts regarding fabric, trim, ratings and costs, prevailing exchange rate trends, wage structures, margin policies including other external and internal factors at hand in order to be able to have an informed sincere discussion.

Other outcomes of the strategy will be the vision of the rationalisation or expansion of suppliers, the projected volume growth by supplier in order to dictate to the supply chain what the capacity requirements are for the both long and short term corresponding periods. This will also include the confirmation of the key mills and fabrications from the raw suppliers closest to the product manufacturers.

Suppliers in new countries in new factories should be researched and identifies taking into account the available capabilities, the legal requirements such as trade restrictions, tariffs and labour regulations. In a similar way potential packaging agencies and suppliers should be identified and researched.

It goes without saying that cost forms an integral part of the negotiation process. It is therefore imperative that the retailer has a good understanding of the components and the proportions of a costing sheet thus permitting the ability to test the validity and understanding of any costing presented by a supplier.

The cost of a product is broken down into two distinct categories, namely direct product costs and the costs associated in getting the completed product to the retailer.

Dynamics that will influence the cost of a product will be the size ratio, which if weighted towards the larger sizes will utilise more fabric or affect the wastage of fabric because of a less efficient marking of the lay of fabric on the cutting table.

The level of detail of the styling may not only affect fabric consumption, it will probably also influence the manufacture time or minute rating.

The width of the fabric can also affect the usage of fabric and the general rule is that the narrower width of fabric the more expensive the product is likely to be. Specialist fabrics tend to be on narrow width such as 110cm while the full width is 148cm. Woven fabrics can be as wide as 160cm.

Plain or printed fabrics will also affect fabric usage particularly where stripes need to be matched on different components such as sleeve and body and is likely to result in more wastage of fabric.

The components of the cost of the products can be divided into those that are considered to be fixed such as raw materials, overheads which include services such as design, technology and logistics and those that are variable which are in the main the constituents that are squeezed down to meet the demands of the retailer like wages, working hours and production methods.

Packaging costs will also vary for different types of product. The size of the cartons required to transport the product is determined by the dimensions of height and width that must protect and accommodate the garment comfortably. The in store presentation requirements will also affect the overall cost from the point of view that allowance may be needed for hangers as well as additional swing tickets.

Where goods are imported, duties need to be taken into consideration. Duties are normally determined against the free on board value or in other words the cost to place it on the deck of the ship. They can also be calculated as ex works which is the cost as at the completion of production.

Exchange rates are a critical element. The option to purchase currency ahead of time at a fixed rate to finance the cost provides the peace of mind that the costs will be stable even if the day to day rates fluctuate. If currency is not bought ahead but goods are purchased at the prevailing rates the retailer may be forced to revise selling prices to ensure the achievement of the target margin.

Different categories of products attract different tariff duties at the receiving country depending on country of origin and manufacture as well as protection policies of local production.

The cost to transport the goods from the place of manufacture will vary for local goods or from the port by the clearing agent, depending on the location of the retailer in relation to the supplier or port, the size of the cartons or container and the mode of transport. Included in this section would be freight and warehousing charges.

The second category can be described as being unrelated to the product directly that have to be paid. The main type of such costs are settlement discount agreements, marketing contributions, finance costs and royalties. These together with the product costs will deliver the final cost of the garment.

Points to note in the review of costs are in cases where the supplier throws in vague and unsubstantiated reasons to justify increases. It is essential that the retailer tests such requests to ensure they carry merit.

A typical instance is where the statement is made that wages have gone up and a new costing is proposed. A cross check is required to determine the proportion of what labour represents of the total costing.

Where increases are attributed to material increases an effort should be made to investigate the trend in the industry and do some comparisons even if they may be a bit crude. If your research shows that the increase is not in line with the trend, the supplier should be encouraged to find a better source and not to pass on the cost of their inefficiencies.

The use of exchange rate fluctuations to motivate cost price changes is more easily resolved as the average movement can be tracked over a period of time and applied. It is a possibility that in fact there might have been an improvement. Foreign currency could also have an influence depending at what price the supplier or retailer may have covered forward.

If the retailer's volumes are increasing significantly the opportunity exists to negotiate a discount in cost price to share the benefits of the improved scale of efficiencies. A point to note is that while this practice is not discouraged, the smaller retailer may not be able to finance the larger volumes of product or growth based incentives. Even with the benefit of a greater margin, the viability remains to be dependent on the organic growth of the chain, for example, the addition of new stores in order to accommodate the higher buying volumes.

A costing approach which is often employed by retailers is that of requesting appropriate suppliers to tender for a product. In order that this is done fairly and equitably the exact same specifications need to be provided to the potential suppliers. Cross costing comparison between suppliers is a popular option where there are large programmes up for grabs and is unlikely to be used for once off high fashion inputs.

For a retailer to commit to high volume programmes, it is a key requisite that the potential suppliers fulfil some basic requirements in that they must be financially stable, have a reliable track record in terms of delivery performance, provide consistent quality with up to date compliancy audits and will be able to cope with the required volumes which could include the agreement to hold a minimum stock holding. The supplier should also be flexible enough to be able to make styling changes to the product where necessary.

The key stipulations for use with cross costing or tenders which will be provided is a detailed style sheet, comprehensive specifications of fabric and trims, the garment measurements with the range of sizes, volumes, a target cost price, packaging requirements and packing methods, delivery dates or production flow.

To achieve a situation where both parties benefit, requires maturity, a clear understanding of the end objectives with informed discussions by both parties and the development of a plan to achieve a mutual objective.

Packaging strategy

The packaged presentation of the product needs to be done in the most pleasing way and must meet the overall design and product standards as set out in the respective guidelines.

Because purchases are emotionally important, clear communication throughout the purchasing process is critical, the message should convey an aesthetic, value for money and ecological consideration that appeals to the customer.

The design of primary packaging must be complimentary in theme across all the different ranges while remaining functional, secure, cost efficient, environmentally friendly and informative.

The strategy for packaging needs to be an all-encompassing one so that there is consistency across the brand values, corporate design and colours of the company. Ideally a standardised process should be in place with clear roles and accountabilities in terms of design, briefing and tracking of development progress as well as for the resolution of issues.

Packaging development and procurement is more often than not quite costly and therefore is frequently a point of tension between the commercial arm and the packaging department in order to keep expense to a minimum. For this reason there is the need for a complete and clear packaging budget policy.

Efficient critical path management of packaging is crucial to ensure that the deadlines in terms of concept approval, design, printing, manufacturing, technological approval and final delivery are aligned to meet the product critical dates and thereby ensure that deliveries are not compromised.

The packaging of a product is largely the responsibility of a packaging technologist and plays a critical role in the presentation, protection and communication of information to the consumer as well as taking into account the ecological demands of the environment.

The common purpose of packaging is that it physically protects the product against mechanical shocks, vibrations, varying temperatures, humidity and excessive handling during transit or warehousing. The usual provision of information whether it is on the packaging itself or through the use of labels, indicate any regulations that may apply, the usage and safety instructions, transport guidelines and lists the components and chemicals that were used in the production process.

Packaging assists in the sale of the product in that it serves as a "silent salesman". There is a communication of information through clever graphic design that encompasses the properties of the product, instructions as how to use the merchandise and the provision of safety warnings. Convenience is added by way of easy storage configurations, display conformity and the accommodation of barcoding information which is easily accessible for scanners to capture sales and stock keeping records and store them on a common data base.

Specialised packaging plays an important part in securing the product through the use of tamper proof mechanisms and can also be engineered to reduce the pilferage.

Over packaging should be avoided and where possible the utilisation of recycled or recyclable materials in the manufacturing process is encouraged without affecting the functional properties.

Outer cartons must adhere to weight and dimension stipulations and should be able to be easily handled on warehouse equipment such as conveyer belts, pallets and storage slots.

Of the two types, primary packaging enjoys the journey of the product right to the end user while secondary packaging is that which is discarded at various points during the journey.

Examples of primary packaging are self- adhesive tickets which carry the barcode detail, price, reference numbers, colour and size as well as date codes. Swing tickets are used where adhesive tickets are not appropriate and may also be independently attached in order to highlight any unique features of the product. Invariably adhesive tickets are applied to presentation packs, wallets and plastic bags.

Sew in labels are typically a satin tape which is sewn into the garment side or neck seam and carry wash care instructions, product reference numbers, size information, fabric composition, country of origin as well as safety instructions. The fibre content must be described by its generic name but may be accompanied by a brand name or a trade mark. An example would be where woollen products will display the wool mark for which the supplier will have qualified to utilise through their manufacturing process.

An example of garment care and reference label

EXAMPLE OF A GARMENT CARE AND REFERENCE LABEL

Care markings are not legally required but are commonly indicated by the universal symbols that are consistent and accurate, for example, where a garment needs to be hand washed only and not machine washed it will be highlighted using the relevant symbol

Universal care instruction symbols are key to the garment label and the most common are outlined below

⌷80°	WASHING WATER TEMPERATURE	⊠	DO NOT TUMBLE DRY
⌷	HAND WASH ONLY	⧄	DRIP DRY IN SHADE
⌷	WASH ON SENSITIVE PROGRAMMES	⊞	DRIP DRY
⊠	DO NOT WASH	⊟	DRY FLAT
Ⓟ	DRY CLEANABLE	⬚	DRY ON HANGER
⊗	DO NOT DRY CLEAN	⊠	DO NOT IRON
⋈	DO NOT USE BLEACH	⌂	IRON WITH WARM IRON
⊠	DO NOT TUMBLE DRY	⌂	IRON WITH HOT IRON

Country of origin is displayed on labels to indicate geographically where the significant stage of production took place. In most countries this is a legal requirement even if the garment may have some components that originate from other parts of the world. Apart from it being law, the identification gives the consumer the choice of which countries that they may wish to support or not support for political or emotional reasons and participate in buy local promotional campaigns that are designed to stimulate local employment.

Swing tags that describe features or unique properties of products have to be truthful in terms of fit for purpose and of the quality standard that is expected by the customer. Where the product does not meet these claims they can be deemed to be misleading and could have legal implications that can be enforced either by the user or competitors who may feel unfairly disadvantaged. An example of this could be that where a ticket describes the garment as being non-iron but after a few washes it has to be ironed.

Secondary packaging are items such as outer cartons, over bags for hanging product, hanger size indicators, stock room and store address labels, the outer carton product detail and supplier detail stamps. Transit cartons or hanging formats need to be protective in order to preserve the quality specifications and make sure that the presentation standards are well maintained. The form and function of the product has to be safeguarded in a cost effective way while conforming to all legal requirements.

The procuring and specifying of ecologically friendly packaging should always be done keeping the safety of the environs top of mind. Printing should be done keeping volatile compound emissions to a minimum through, for example, the use of vegetable based ink that are free from heavy metals.

Measures need to be put in place to keep waste of inks, ink tins, and paper to a minimum and the cleaning and recirculation of polluted water should be promoted. Paper packaging and corrugated cartons ought to contain a percentage of recycled papers and must not to have been bleached using chlorine. Plastic packaging should be of recyclable materials such as polypropylene and polyethylene.

Logistical strategy

The logistical approach to best serve the stores requires options which effectively deliver the goods to the customer from diverse sources at cost efficient rates, as quickly as possible, while maintaining the integrity and quality of the goods.

For the movement of product from a supplier through an arrangement of regional warehouses enables deliveries to be closer to the retailer's outlets. This may take on the method whereby the supplier delivers to a number of regional warehouses throughout the country, which receives and stores the goods awaiting allocation instructions from the commercial office that trigger a pick and pack operation prior to distribution to the stores in the respective area.

Storage and the distribution operations in a central warehouse are normally situated in the major centres where the acceptance of the delivery takes place from suppliers who are in the closest proximity. Once the allocation instructions are received the product is picked and packed prior to distribution to local stores. For those stores that do not fall in the service area of the receiving warehouse the goods are trunked in bulk to other geographical locations where the pick and pack function will be actioned and thereby ultimately all the stores throughout the country are catered for.

Much of the volume of stock held in the warehouse is received ahead of the season and the frequency of deliveries may well depend on factors such as minimum order quantities, pack sizes, proximity of suppliers, particularly in the case of off shore manufacturers.

Distribution models also exist where there is a flow through consolidation at distribution centres and the physical storage of the product is pushed back up the supply chain to the manufacturer. Allocation instructions are communicated to the supplier to enable the product to be picked, packed and labelled at individual store level which is then delivered to a distribution centre. Consolidation of the cartons from all suppliers takes place at store level to await dispatch. The advantage of this format is that the handling of product is minimised and the cost of storage for the retailer is reduced.

Movement of overseas manufactured goods is done in the main through freight and forwarding agents who manage off shore consolidation points. Suppliers deliver containers or part deliveries to these facilities and the agent will implement the logistical arrangements for the merging of the goods for retailers prior to dispatch via sea or air. In some instances the goods may be picked, packed and labeled at this facility ready for distribution to stores upon arrival as is done with local suppliers. However, this is really only practical for once off or initial deliveries and does not suit follow up or continuity replenishment orders.

Critical to the efficient movement of product will be that of ensuring the correct documentation and tariffs are all in place in order to facilitate the free flow of product through customs and excise. Once the goods arrive in the destination country they are cleared and delivered to the retailer. Thereafter the same process is followed as for the local suppliers and in all likelihood utilises the model where goods are delivered to a central warehouse which will be in the city of the port where the goods have been offloaded.

Supply chain logistics is described as the product movement comprising of the transport and shipment of goods from the point of origination and clearance through customs where applicable to the distribution centre or warehouse and on to stores where the goods are placed on offer for purchase to the customer. Many stores traditionally have stockroom facilities or at least a backroom to accommodate overflow stocks.

The reality is that the same rates of rental are charged as that for saleable metreage and therefore it is preferable that off-site storage facilities be maintained. The downside of holding stocks in high rental cost stock rooms is that invariably the remnant stocks of promotions or themes are removed from the sales floor and left in the stock room to gather dust waiting for the seasonal write down.

Out of season stocks such as thermal underwear are returned to the stockroom to await the reappearance of the next season to be returned to the sales floor. In such situations, particularly where there are undisciplined controls in the store, stocks get lost in the black hole of the stock room and bad or dead stock will accumulate and affect the data integrity of the stock records. It is therefore essential that redundant stocks are written off and cleared out almost immediately.

The trend is to keep store holding areas as small as possible and enable the regular drawing off from larger economical offsite storage facilities which can be done more effectively through a centralised point whether it be at the warehouse or in the commercial office. The success as to how well this is done is dependent on the responsiveness of the warehouse and reduces the accumulation of isolated pockets of stocks while minimising the corruption of stock data integrity as well as the reduction of double handling of merchandise.

Examples of stock held in the holding room is the accommodation of an overflow of stock where space planning is applied using planograms. End of ranges stock that have to be returned to the centralised storage facility or supplier may need to be held temporarily in the back room awaiting collection. Stock is also temporarily held for consolidation in back room areas until all components of a promotional launch is received and moved to the sales floor on the launch date for maximum impact.

The selection of the various options of supply chain will depend on a number of criteria such as the source of supply, characteristics of the product, the costs of the storage and distribution, selling locations, shelf life and customer demand.

The main channels of supply are a flow through model without storage or warehoused product. Outside of these channels the other formats are direct delivery to stores or displays being fully merchandised by the vendor.

The type of distribution model that is selected will depend on factors such as the size and growth phase of the retailer. For example, smaller or new retailers will probably prefer to operate a cross dock model which does not require investment in large warehouse facilities or the need to carry excessive inventory enabling their efforts to be focused possibly on opening more stores.

For a larger mature retail chain on the other hand, it may be essential to operate through a network of sophisticated warehousing facilities. These enjoy elaborate systems whereby they have better control of the management of the inventory and are able to efficiently allocate, pick and pack and schedule deliveries to stores country wide or even internationally.

Retailers also have the choice to manage their own facilities or outsource them. The main factor that is considered in selecting the most suitable option is the cost saving element. Initially it may have been cheaper to outsource without having to invest in the high setup cost of such an infra-structure, however, as the retailer grows, coupled to the fact that the third party is a profit based operation that delivers expertise in the warehousing field, the time will come when it is more beneficial to move the operation in house.

A workable compromise solution that is often employed is for the retailer to control their own warehouse facilities with the accompanying IT infrastructure and avoid the major upheaval should they change third parties but to still outsource the transport network part to specialised haulage service providers.

Cross dock or flow through model is the arrangement where the goods are pre picked and packed at the supplier and are delivered to the distribution centre with store labels already gummed on the boxes or hanging sets. The alternative model of cross dock is where the order across the stores is delivered in bulk by the supplier to the cross dock facility and the goods are picked by distribution centre staff and deposited directly in the respective store dispatch bays. Eventually the product from all suppliers for the day is consolidated in each store's designated bay awaiting transport.

Stores that are geographically far from the receiving distribution centre have the goods transhipped in bulk to their own respective closest geographical distribution centre where the picking operation will take place. The number of regional distribution centres will be largely dependent on the density of the store network and the operating costs of such facilities.

The added benefit of the goods being picked and packed at the supplier is that the cartons are able to contain a combination of size and colour requirements by store and will therefore eliminate the need to unpack and repack from warehouse stock thus eliminating double handling and is subsequently more cost efficient. It is also possible where the supplier is picking multiple styles for the same store that these can be nested in the same container which reduces the need for additional packaging as well as reduces handling making for a considerable time saving.

In the event that there are over or short deliveries these cause delays as the changed quantity requires that the computer is updated and the store quantities are scaled or recalculated based on varying algorithms that satisfy those stores with the greatest need first rather than simply apportioning equally across all the stores before the picking process can take place.

In the case where the receipt of product from suppliers is pre labelled for stores the testing of the accuracy is done by randomly inspecting a sample of cartons per supplier delivery and should the errors of packing fall outside of a certain tolerance it may result in the entire delivery being rejected. Where inaccuracies are within the tolerance but there is still a measure of incorrectness the error factor will still be extrapolated for the entire delivery and the invoicing is amended accordingly. Dependent on the size of the error it could attract a penalty. While many find this concept difficult to accept, it should be remembered that the time and cost to do a full unpack and reconciliation in all likelihood would render the operation to be considered impracticable. Tests have been statistically done which reveal that the deviation from the sample survey results is also not that large.

The advantage of a flow through supply chain type is that the allocation can be made as late as possible allowing the shortening of the lead time and thereby meeting the customer demand more efficiently. The other benefit is also that the storage space requirement is minimal and dependent on the payment obligation it may be beneficial to the retailer in terms of cash flow in that ownership is only transferred upon receipt at the distribution centre.

There is an argument that utilising cross dock without warehousing is possibly a disadvantage in terms of the speed of delivery to stores as having stock drawn from the warehouse is quicker and smoother than waiting for the supplier delivery. The challenge is therefore to streamline the supplier delivery efficiencies to avoid the cost impact of holding warehoused stock and the handling costs that accompany this option.

Other difficult situations arise where there is a poor performing unreliable supplier for which a contingency is required when they fail to deliver and similarly at key periods such as holidays where the factories shut down for a period and in spite of confirming that there will be a skeleton staff to cope with the execution of orders over this period the level of service is invariably diminished.

Example of a cross dock flow through model

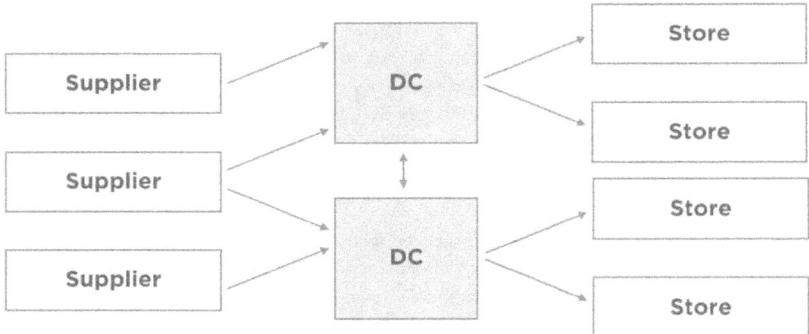

Warehoused product is where the goods are received in bulk and are held in storage awaiting a call off and distribution to stores or to other storage sheds using the cross dock facilities.

The warehouse can be seen to operate in a similar way as the supplier and performance management of indicators such as pick and pack accuracy, lead time measurement and the like can be implemented in the same way.

Warehoused stock tends to be predominantly for imported product but can also include local suppliers particularly where minimum order quantities or negotiated special volume deals apply. In the main the products are continuity items with long supply lead times which are replenished on a regular basis as "pull" allocations.

The challenge with warehouse stock is to manage the stock levels as the investment in high volumes does not only have adverse financial consequences but also a real physical problem can arise in the form of space constraints and the possible requirement of additional operational resources. There are also instances of seasonal goods such as knitwear being produced in the off season to maintain a consistent production throughout the year and therefore creates an accumulation of stocks in the warehouse either at the supplier or the retailer at a cost which needs to be accounted for.

A point to note is that the storage shelving location is restricted to a fixed size which is usually the size of a pallet and may be at multi levels. As goods are withdrawn to the pick and pack locations it does happen that within one storage location a lesser quantity of goods remain behind which results in the space utilisation not being optimal as two different SKU's are not able to share the same location. Technically the warehouse becomes restricted in the capacity availability while physically this may not be the case. Thought needs to be applied to the minimum percentage or quantity that is able to be efficiently maintained and what tactics must be utilised regarding the consolidation of and removal of such stocks to free up the storage slots. This may take the form of allocating the odds to stores or transferring it to a different storage area with smaller slots and take on a high priority for distribution thereafter.

Other space inhibiting practices are where there are poor rates of sales, or volume deals are negotiated or through minimum order quantities that are imposed which cause the warehouses to fill up eventually and consequently result in the total utilisation of palette slots. The alternative then remains to either source outside storage, put the brakes on in terms of accepting intake or to simply stop buying to relieve the space and financial strain. The consequences of this is that availabilities suffer with the disruption of the composition of product and theme launches as well as the service levels of suppliers decline when they put production on hold while they wait for the retailer's stock levels to diminish and inevitably will sell on to other competitors in order to keep their production capacity full and operational.

The siting and the number of warehouses will be reliant on the geographic network of stores, the proximity to suppliers and ports and will be dependent on the achievement of the most economical costs which need to be continually reviewed to ensure the delicate balance of viability is maintained. This balance is particularly important in the case of retail chains which continually open and close stores.

The introduction of higher levels of automation and the possibility of outsourcing operations to contractors or independent logistical organisations for storage and the management of the fleet of transport to tranship between storage points and schedule deliveries to stores also has an impact on the sustainability.

After the unloading of a container or truck at the back door, the cartons are consolidated and received, and then palletized for packing away in the storage facilities with unique identification location barcodes for ease of retrieval upon withdrawal in bulk.

After drawing product in bulk from the shelves the goods are moved to a pick and pack location to satisfy each stores order and are deposited in the unique store bays to await dispatch.

An alternative option is to pick and pack goods directly from storage shelves by store and when the order of the various products for each specific store is complete it is delivered to the store's relevant bay.

The appropriateness of which picking method to apply will depend largely on the size of the withdrawals. The larger volumes are usually removed to a picking area in bulk where the pick and pack operations take place. The smaller the quantities that are required by store, the picking by individual store across the product range into picking bins or shipping units for each store would probably be more suitable. It is possible that some retailer's employ both methods from different areas of the warehouse dependent on the product characteristics and volumes.

The task of picking is activated by the generation of a computer picking sheet which informs the picker as to which location must be accessed and indicates the quantity that must be withdrawn. Together with this the computer will create the store labels which is applied to the shipping container.

There are generally two methods of generating picking lists and labels. The more manual method is where the picking lists are generated up front prior to the picking operation but the downside is that it is susceptible to inaccuracies and at the end of the operation the computer needs to be updated manually and report any exceptions. The implication is that this step must be fulfilled before any goods can be shipped which could cause delays.

The other option is real time picking which is the technique of using hand held terminals that employ radio frequency to give the pickers their instructions on a computer terminal or pad. With the handheld terminal or voice instructions via hands free headsets the picker will scan the barcodes of the product and locations to confirm that the correct product has been identified and the picking can commence which will then update the stock data base in real time. For this reason the accuracy   is almost guaranteed and the movement of stock is free flowing.

As all retailers are concerned about shrinkage this method is a big plus and also lessens the possibility of disputes between the warehouse and stores with respect to over or short deliveries. The facility to automatically generate store delivery notes is provided enabling the deliveries to be tracked. Real time control does however come at a much added cost and therefore the viability must be assessed in terms of the benefits it brings with it.

There are sophisticated automated picking systems which lessen the manual handling of product but these require a higher level of investment. The most common system employed is a conveyer belt system whereby the pickers are relatively stationery and are responsible for a section of products in an area where the items are packed onto the conveyer belt from which picking takes place and can be done for either the store or product picking options.

Challenges that the picking operation faces is that different approaches are required to segment activities in cases where fast selling items need to be picked more frequently and others such as for some stores that require less service than others. Consequently there is a prerequisite to carefully schedule actions in order to streamline deliveries.

In a similar way the peaks and valleys of volumes through the week apply undue strain on the operation at certain times while at other spells the warehouse may stand idle. In the case of clothing where there are not many expiry dates involved the approach should possibly be to pick the high volume product outside the peak delivery periods and reserve the ability to prioritise the promotion items during the peak delivery period thereby smoothing the operation and maintain a constant labour utilisation.

The ideal size of the warehouse is difficult to assess but the general rule is obviously the smaller the warehouse the better as the overheads are kept to a minimum and experience often shows whatever the size of the shed is it will inevitably be filled. The size should be tailored to the space required during normal trading and not to accommodate peak periods such as Christmas or the accumulation of stock build up prior to Chinese New Year when at such times additional temporary space can possibly be procured or alternatively implement night shifts to keep stocks moving.

The flow of product within a warehouse environment is illustrated below

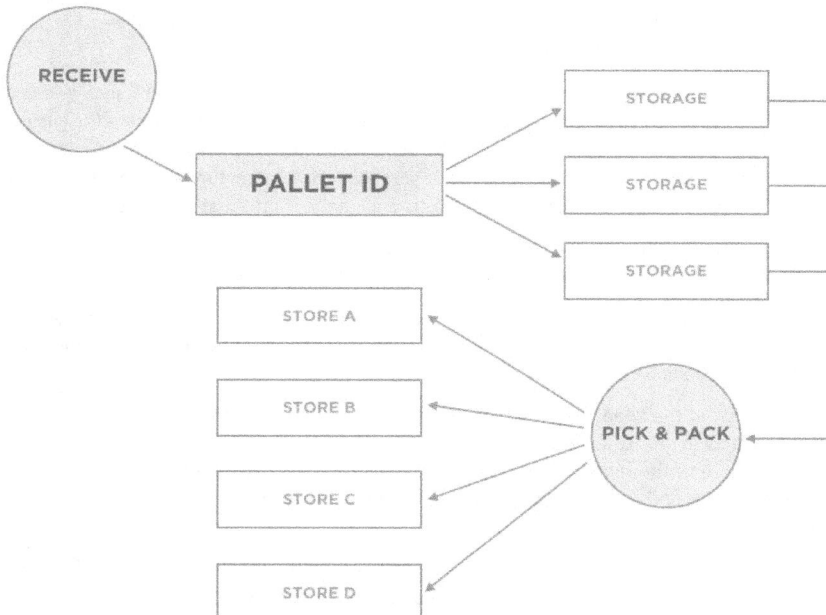

Direct delivery of product to the store location by the supplier is used where the retailer does not have the infrastructure to accommodate certain types of product such as high priced goods like cosmetics and expensive accessories.

This mode of delivery is also required where the vendor completes the end to end merchandising management of the displays whereby slow selling stock is withdrawn and replaced by the supplier. A typical example would be a product such as greeting cards, accessories and magazines.

In summary, a well-managed supply chain enables the retailer to acquire goods from the manufacturer more profitably, facilitate well controlled stock levels, and provide more timeous response to the consumer demand as well as the building of sustainable working relationships between the retailer and the supplier.

Value added processing occurs in the main when the need for additional work on product is frequent and the facilities to do this has to be provided for to make goods store ready. The nature of value added work can take on a variety of forms but typical examples are as follows.

Goods that are received from off shore suppliers may be bulk packed or not be received in their final form in order to achieve optimum space utilisation during transit. Prime examples of this is in the case of cushions or duvets which are space hungry but are relatively light. In order to accomplish the most efficient space usage these goods may be transported without the fibre filling or alternatively are vacuum packed. However, this operation then creates the need for additional work upon receipt to fill the cushions and unpacking of the vacuum packs as well as treating the product through pressing or steaming.

The transport of goods in cartons that eventually will be displayed on hangers, such as men's formal suits or ladies tailored garments, is done to maximise the space efficiency in containers. Upon arrival they will need to be unpacked and placed on hangers and will have to be steamed either with a hand steamer or pass through a steam tunnel. In most cases this will also require the attachment of price tickets and garment information labels.

Repackaging may be required where bulk transit quantities need to be debagged and repackaged into smaller stock room packs ready for allocation to stores.

It does happen that there may be garments received from the supplier with defects or returned from stores which are repairable in order to make them available in a saleable state which has to be done by the value-adder.

The location of the added value service provider can be either at an independent site or be incorporated in the retailer's warehouse facility. The challenge with an offsite location, particularly with the receipt of offshore product is the fact that the goods are received by another facility and reflect on a separate stock record which renders the administration of stock to be more complex.

It is preferable to have the value added processing done in the retailer's warehouse facility as there is control of the receipt of the goods and performance is more easily managed. The operation can possibly be done on a contractual basis whereby the processor rents space within the warehouse or the space is alternatively staffed with warehouse resources as a separate entity and not included in the distribution centre operational costs. It should be noted that the cost of this processing work forms part of the cost of the product and must be included in the determination of the product margin.

The costing structures for work done is a complex one as the type of work is not always consistent and therefore needs to be broken down into some detail.

Value added costing would typically consist of a basic cost for the overheads and handling of the product which is usually relatively stable but may vary depending on the type of product being processed. Charges per operation such as a rate per garment for steaming, labelling, placing on hangers and the like will be added to the base costs. Out of the ordinary operations such as ad hoc repairs will be dependent on the results of negotiation between the processor and the buying departments.

The method of transport will be determined by a number of criteria. The option for clothing is either in cartons or in the form of hanging sets. The choice is dependent mainly on the characteristic of the product, the cost comparison between the two models and the equipment infra-structure of the supplier and distribution centres. Many of the more sophisticated production plants have the overhead rail systems that can accommodate hanging goods and which can facilitate the transport of the goods hanging from rails affixed to the ceiling of the vehicle to the retailer.

The cost of the hanging storage and transport of product will come at added expense for the rail systems in comparison to the charge for distribution in cartons. The time saving as a cost offset in the case of moving hanging goods needs to be considered and in many cases it is also dependent on the nature of fabrics such as voiles as well as the structure of garments as is the case for formal wear. If crease sensitive goods are moved in cartons there is a need for an added value processing requirement to steam and bag the goods which can either take place at the distribution centre or at the stores upon receipt which comes at an additional cost. The transport of formal wear in cartons could also lead to persistent creases in the garment such as the fold in pants that may be difficult to eradicate even with intense steaming.

Where retailers insist on receiving goods in boxes, a reverse cost may have to be applied where sophisticated manufacturing plants that only cater for hanging goods to maximise the scales of efficiency will need to purchase cartons and employ additional labour to pack the garments into boxes as well as encounter an additional time delay.

The downsides of the hanging format is that the equipment is expensive, space requirement is greater, and where multiple hangers are hung vertically to save space in the outer bag there could be the danger of bunching of longer garments at the bottom of the bag. Space wastage below the hanging bags in the vehicles also needs to be taken into account.

The advantage of time saving that hanging formats deliver in comparison to goods transported in cartons is that goods in cartons have the benefit of easier handling, better space utilization and less capital investment. However the necessity of capacity planning for processing to steam and place products on hangers together with the additional cost, extended lead time and a risk that the quality may be compromised needs to be weighed up.

Another determining factor will be the aesthetics of the garment that may lend it to be displayed on hangers such as casual shirts made from natural fibres or styled tailored goods which will better highlight the features and promote the unique feel of the special fabrics.

Goods are stored and dispatched as hanging sets that will comprise of a fixed number of garments in the same colour and sizes and are allocated as such. This makes for easier handling and loading into vehicles especially where the equipment is able to access the vehicle or container directly from the despatch area.

The optimisation of the supply chain calls for an end to end cost analysis and monitoring to ensure that the goods reach the sales floors efficiently to best service the customer through consistent availability without the congestion of stock in warehouses and back rooms.

A flow diagram which indicates the garment and fibre types which best suit the method of storage, transport and display can be illustrated as follows

Product security Wastage through pilferage is an important factor that needs attention during the movement of the product. Control is done by various methods but mostly through the use of sealed containers, marked sealing tapes on cartons, sample tests of contents in cartons, locked and sealed back doors on trucks and sophisticated handover procedures. There is a breakeven point where the cost to maintain the security must be weighed up against the shrinkage allowance as it may be overkill to secure cheaper products with refined protection. The additional labour and checkpoints will slow down the movement of product through the pipeline as well as lower the service levels and therefore may not make it meaningful. On the other hand it could well be very worthwhile for the movement of high value product.

Marketing strategy

Marketing teams use various types of promotional strategies to effectively expose the product in the most attractive way to the customer. Traditional mechanisms in the form of print, radio, television, in house magazines, local media, flyers, shelf talkers, posters, bill boards, scratch cards and the like are still very prominent.

However in growing magnitudes is the creative use of the electronic channels such as internet, sms, e-mail and social media like face book and twitter.

Together with the increased usage of technology a clear distinction has developed between the brand building objective and that of the management of the retailer's reputation. Some of the larger retailers have put specific management structures in place to perform this task. A reservoir of goodwill needs to grow in order to enhance the reputation in the eyes of the consumer. In the same way that positive comments grow the reputation, negative comments may potentially be as destructive when issues arise but in such cases where the reputation quotient is high there is evidence that the level of criticism is less severe.

The focal points of reputation measurements are how much the retailer stacks up in terms of trust, esteem and admiration for the way they operate in the field of not only the product performance and innovation but also that of their workplace environment, the decent governance they uphold and the moral citizenship they display within the community.

Loyalty programmes are very popular in rewarding the customer either in the form of points, coupons or discounts. Such programmes are not only extremely effective in significantly improving sales and profits but they also permit the retailer to analyse the buying habits of the customer in detail and consequently are able to better service the consumer needs. Programmes also enable the retailer to build a data base through which they can communicate directly with the customer in terms of highlighting special offers, the awarding of gift vouchers for special events such as birthdays through using various mediums such as newsletters, e-mail, social media and the postal service. Examples of such programmes are not only to reward for purchases above a certain amount but may also be for first time buyers, freebies such as buy one get one free while some are targeted at specific categories of product and account holders. The objective of a good loyalty programme strategy should be to attract and keep new relationships, embed positive perceptions of existing customers, heighten brand awareness and not necessarily simply just provide a service for those discount hungry customers who see such incentives as a means to save money.

Social responsibility is incorporated in the marketing strategy in that it displays the commitment to the community, the disadvantaged and the development and welfare of employees in the form of initiatives other than just those which are purely profit motivated.

Conclusion
While a lot has been documented on the subject of strategic planning, the proof of the pudding is in the eating in that the success of the plan is reflected in the sincerity, integrity and results that are delivered.

More often than not after a lot of effort and time by a number of people has been inputted in the formulation of the plan, unless it is applied, measured and adapted it is simply a waste. It is not uncommon for the strategic plan to be left on the shelf and the executive director carries on going in different directions without the board demanding fidelity to the agreed goals. While changing direction may be warranted, these should be carefully vetted and agreed by all stakeholders and the plan amended accordingly.

For this reason it is critical that disciplined check points are established where the actual performance of the plan is measured in terms of its efficiency, the actual deliverance compared to the targets set out, the quality and the flexibility of the plan to be able to adapt easily.

A key focus in the assessment of the past performance for the season is to compare the actual key numbers to that what was expected and understand the deviations whether they were positive or negative. The learnings are imperative in the compilation of a new season's strategy and setting of targets.

The key topics that need to be questioned and evaluated are:

Product

- Were the trends which were anticipated in line with what actually materialised? What needs to be taken into account when predicting the future season's trends?
- Did the strategy that was set for the brand and customer together with that of the group and department as well as the supplier selection deliver the envisaged objectives? What needs to be done differently for the new season?

Customers and competitors

- Did the information on customer segmentation and the action plans cater effectively in the satisfaction of the needs? What adaptations and additional resources are needed for the future season?
- Did the competitor initiatives which were anticipated actually happen and was it possible to effectively counteract them? What other methodologies are available to keep up to date with the market place activities?

Key performance indicators

- Were the targets of sales, margins, stock levels and turns, gross and net profits achieved as per plan or were they unrealistic? What measures require review and which activities are needed to be put in place to achieve them in the new season?
- Was the product assortment in the right proportions and did they perform to acceptable levels to cater for all customer segments effectively? Were the product innovations and promotions that were implemented successful and at the right levels?
- What were the actual colours and sizes sold in comparison to the volumes purchased and what should have been bought instead?
- Identify product sales which need to be adjusted to a realistic level as a result of product failure, poor availabilities and any other factors such as competitive activity and what special events were there that may have influenced sales either positively or negatively.

Suppliers

- Did the suppliers perform to the levels that maximised availability in the right quantities and on time?
- Did the selected suppliers possess the right capabilities to deliver the programmes that were allotted in terms of innovation, complexity, capacity, quality and on time delivery? Are there other suppliers who should be considered?
- Was the feedback received from suppliers of a nature that can help improve the working relationships going forward?

Stores

- Were stores able to understand the structure of the ranges and easily display them to emphasize the thinking of the buying team? What improvements to guidelines can be made to assist them?
- Was the feedback received from stores valuable and what mechanisms can be implemented to improve the quality of feedback?

Marketing

- Were the marketing channels that were utilised effective and was the uplift in sales able to be measured accurately against control products? Which other communication mediums would be considered?
- Were the promotions successful and what was the extent of substitution purchases?
- What was the feedback from store staff and customers?
- Were the social initiative objectives achieved?

In the final analysis if the responses to the above evaluation points are positive one can safely say that an effective strategy was applied. If some of the results were not as those that were expected the key is to take the lessons learnt on board and focus on them in the preparation for future seasons.

In summary, having a farsighted view of the overall big picture of the retail environment, with an all-inclusive attention to detail and being aware of early warning signs to effectively avoid challenges through the optimised use of the tools, mechanisms and talents at hand is without doubt a key factor in delivering a successful and sustainable retail business.

110

INDEX

A

added value · 90
agent · 55, 78, 83
allocation · 32, 47, 48, 50, 55, 75, 83, 85, 90
Allocation instructions · 83
allocator · 32
Analysis options · 52
assortment · 41, 93
attributes · 25, 68
availabilities · 46, 72, 87, 93

B

balance · 33, 39, 41, 42, 43, 44, 49, 51, 52, 53, 66, 87
barcodes · 74, 87
Behavioural influences · 34
better value goods · 24
blends of fibres · 67
blog · 36
brand · 20, 24, 25, 30, 36, 52, 53, 61, 62, 80, 81, 92, 93
Brand · 24
budgets · 30, 31, 37, 38
Business unit · 23
buyer · 29, 30, 31, 38, 41
buying · 5, 24, 26, 27, 28, 29, 31, 32, 38, 39, 41, 49, 52, 53, 54, 55, 56, 63, 66, 67, 68, 69, 72, 76, 80, 87, 90, 92, 94, 99
Buying Margin · 20

C

capabilities · 55, 56, 64, 67, 68
cartons · 61, 78, 80, 82, 83, 85, 87, 90, 91
categories · 20, 31, 39, 41, 49, 69, 78, 92
category · 28, 29, 31, 39, 45, 67, 79
chains · 19, 72, 73, 87
change · 6, 19, 20, 51, 52, 55, 71, 74, 85
choices · 29, 41, 43
colour · 28, 31, 32, 35, 36, 37, 38, 39, 41, 43, 44, 45, 46, 47, 48, 52, 55, 62, 68, 74, 75, 81, 85, 91
commercial acumen · 30
commercial team · 67
commitment · 51, 66, 83, 92
communication · 24, 30, 56, 60, 62, 80, 92, 94
competitive price · 67
competitiveness · 30, 74
competitors · 15, 19, 25, 55, 82, 87
consolidation points · 83

D

container · 55, 78, 85, 87, 91
continuity · 41, 43, 47, 48, 49, 86
co-ordination · 43
core · 24, 36, 41, 43, 44, 47, 53, 55, 56, 75
costing · 30, 54, 57, 75, 78, 79, 90
crease · 67
critical milestone management · 31
critical path management · 6, 27, 32, 61, 80
cross dock · 84, 85, 86
customer · 5, 7, 15, 20, 24, 25, 26, 29, 30, 31, 32, 33, 34, 35, 36, 37, 38, 39, 41, 42, 43, 44, 45, 50, 52, 57, 61, 69, 71, 72, 73, 74, 80, 82, 83, 84, 85, 91, 92, 93
customer profiles · 24, 29, 34, 72
Customer returns · 61, 75
customer segments · 33, 93
customers · 20, 25, 29, 33, 36, 38, 39, 41, 43, 44, 45, 49, 52, 71, 72, 73, 94
customs · 83

D

data · 24, 32, 48, 49, 60, 72, 74, 80, 84, 88, 92
data integrity · 49, 72, 84
deadlines · 29, 32, 54, 56, 75, 80
decreases · 43
delivery · 11, 33, 48, 52, 53, 55, 56, 57, 61, 64, 66, 67, 75, 79, 80, 83, 84, 85, 88, 89, 94
delivery dates · 33, 64, 79, 80
demographics · 24, 35, 45, 73
department · 27, 31, 32, 43, 45, 56, 74, 93
depth · 41
design · 29, 36, 42, 43, 52, 53, 54, 56, 62, 63, 66, 68, 69, 74, 78, 80
Designers · 29
destination · 36, 61, 83
development · 32, 36, 38, 67, 69, 71, 80, 92
discount · 20, 43, 44, 72, 73, 75, 79, 92
display space · 30
displays · 74, 84, 89, 92
Displays · 74
distribution centre · 55, 83, 84, 85, 90
distribution centres · 72, 83, 85, 90
distributor · 32

E

easy care · 67, 70
easy to iron · 67
efficiencies · 54, 68, 74, 79, 85
elastane · 67

emerging markets · 24, 73
emotional maturity · 30, 31
environmentally friendly · 80
exchange rate · 7, 55, 65, 77, 79
expenses · 73

F

fabric · 29, 30, 43, 53, 62, 64, 65, 67, 68, 70, 77, 78, 79, 81
Fabric · 67, 69
Fabric technologists · 67
fabrics · 24, 30, 53, 66, 67, 68, 69, 70, 75, 78, 90, 91
factory · 35, 61, 67, 73
fashion blogs · 36
fashionability · 25, 42, 70
fibres · 67, 70, 71, 91
Fibres · 70
financial targets · 38
finishing · 67
fitting rooms · 36
flow through · 83, 84, 86
forecasting · 29, 30, 32
form and function · 30, 41, 67, 68, 82
forward planning · 31, 32
forward stock covers · 31
forwarding agents · 83
Franchise · 73
fringe · 41
functionality · 42, 52, 80

G

garment · 29, 30, 42, 53, 54, 55, 62, 64, 65, 67, 68, 74, 77, 78, 79, 81, 82, 90, 91
Generation Y · 36
gift vouchers · 92
goals · 24, 36, 37, 38
governance · 92
groups · 24, 28, 44, 52, 76

H

handles · 67
handling of product · 83, 88
hanging sets · 85, 90, 91

I

incentives · 74, 75, 79, 92
increases · 43, 79
information systems · 32
initiatives · 24, 52, 55, 92, 93
innovate · 20, 36

innovation · 20, 24, 55, 56, 65, 67, 68, 69, 75, 77, 92, 94
Innovation · 67, 68
input · 24, 26, 37, 38, 47
inspection · 60, 67
intake · 31, 38, 41, 43, 46, 47, 50, 87
internet · 24, 29, 36, 49, 71, 92
inventory · 55, 74, 84

K

knitted · 67

L

Late deliveries · 75
launches · 35, 47, 87
Lead times · 75
leaders · 19, 23
lifestyle · 20, 24, 28, 33, 52, 74
like to like · 43
local · 36, 45, 53, 54, 55, 78, 82, 83, 85, 86, 92
local suppliers · 83
location · 28, 32, 35, 36, 73, 78, 86, 87, 89, 90
logistical · 27, 32, 54, 61, 62, 66, 69, 83, 87
logistics · 6, 27, 54, 62, 78, 83
loyal · 20
loyalty · 24, 35, 36, 92
Loyalty programmes · 72, 92

M

Malls · 73
manual · 48, 49, 60, 61, 62, 87, 88
margin · 30, 38, 43, 44, 65, 75, 77, 78, 79, 90
markdowns · 31
Markdowns · 20
market share · 24, 39
marketing · 24, 25, 27, 33, 41, 62, 73, 79, 92
Marketing · 36, 72, 92
measurements · 26, 48, 72, 74, 76, 92
measures · 21, 52, 59, 69, 93
meeting · 28, 29, 30, 42, 44, 52, 57, 66, 68, 75, 85
meetings · 32, 62, 65, 76
merchandiser · 31, 32, 33
merchandising · 5, 27, 30, 31, 53, 89, 99
mills · 54, 59, 67, 68, 69, 75
minimum order quantities · 53, 55, 83, 86, 87
models · 20, 34, 56, 83, 90
movement · 43, 75, 79, 83, 88, 89, 91

N

Negotiating · 65
Negotiation · 65

new lines · 48
newness · 41, 44, 74

O

off shore · 24, 53, 54, 55, 61, 66, 83, 89
offer · 20, 31, 38, 39, 53, 56, 66, 71, 72, 73, 75, 84
offshore · 54, 55, 62, 83, 90
on line · 24, 36, 72
Online · 71
open to buy · 31
operational plan · 6
operational plans · 24, 32
opportunities · 6, 24, 25, 26, 31, 39, 52, 65, 67, 68, 73
order · 20, 25, 30, 31, 35, 36, 38, 39, 41, 43, 44, 45, 49,
    51, 53, 54, 55, 60, 61, 62, 65, 67, 68, 69, 72, 74, 75,
    77, 79, 82, 83, 85, 86, 87, 88, 90, 92
Order fill · 76
ordering · 27, 32
organisational structures · 32
organisations · 20, 87
overstocks · 49

P

pack sizes · 83
packaging · 24, 27, 33, 36, 53, 61, 62, 64, 68, 75, 79, 80,
    81, 82, 83, 85
Packaging · 61, 78, 80
Pareto principle · 11
part deliveries · 83
Pay points · 74
penalties · 33, 62, 74, 75, 76
percentage · 66, 75, 76, 83, 86
perception · 5, 25, 29, 34, 43
performance · 20, 21, 24, 26, 30, 32, 35, 37, 38, 47, 48,
    49, 50, 51, 52, 56, 60, 61, 62, 66, 69, 70, 74, 75, 76,
    79, 86, 90, 92, 93
peripheral lines · 41
picking · 55, 60, 61, 72, 85, 87, 88
pipeline · 51, 92
plan · 5, 6, 7, 15, 19, 24, 31, 33, 36, 37, 38, 41, 45, 46, 47,
    50, 51, 52, 65, 67, 79, 93
planning · 6, 11, 16, 32, 36, 37, 38, 39, 45, 47, 48, 50, 57,
    68, 84, 91
Planning · 7
potential · 5, 7, 19, 24, 34, 39, 49, 51, 55, 56, 66, 67, 75,
    76, 79
presentation · 30, 78, 80, 82
Presentation of scenarios · 11
price · 25, 35, 38, 41, 43, 44, 52, 53, 64, 65, 66, 77, 79,
    81, 90
pricing · 31, 39, 43, 44, 52, 62, 66
principles · 5, 6, 41
problem resolution · 31
product mix · 26, 36, 37, 38, 39

production · 11, 29, 30, 32, 37, 38, 46, 47, 52, 53, 54, 55,
    56, 57, 61, 62, 65, 66, 67, 68, 69, 70, 71, 75, 78, 79,
    80, 82, 86, 87
profile · 25, 31, 33, 35, 39, 45
profiles · 34, 45, 73
profit · 28, 30, 39, 49, 68, 84, 92
profitability · 31, 65, 67, 77
profits · 28, 31, 32, 72, 92, 93
promotional · 35, 43, 66, 74, 82, 84
Protection · 62
psychological needs · 35
public relations · 25, 36

Q

quality · 20, 30, 31, 33, 52, 53, 54, 55, 56, 57, 62, 63, 65,
    66, 67, 68, 73, 75, 79, 82, 83, 91, 94
Quality controllers · 67

R

range plan · 31, 37, 38, 39, 41, 43
range structure · 42
ranges · 25, 29, 30, 31, 39, 41, 44, 66, 71, 80, 94
rate of sale · 47
rationalisation · 43, 77
raw materials · 54, 61, 67, 78
regional warehouse · 83
regional warehousing · 83
remuneration · 57, 68, 75
Repackaging · 90
replenishment · 48, 55, 83
reports · 21, 32, 47, 60, 61, 69, 76
reputation · 92
research · 6, 24, 30, 41, 79
responsibility · 28, 55, 59, 67, 68, 80
Retailers · 36, 84
retailing · 5, 74
Return on Inventory Investment · 20
reviews · 30, 60
right product · 39

S

safety · 57, 59, 62, 64, 69, 70, 80, 81, 82
sales · 11, 24, 30, 31, 32, 38, 39, 46, 47, 48, 49, 51, 52,
    55, 60, 61, 72, 73, 74, 75, 76, 80, 84, 87, 91, 92, 93,
    94
Sales · 20, 37, 38
Sales Margin · 20
sales performance · 76
sales value · 38
sampling · 67
season · 24, 26, 30, 31, 37, 38, 41, 43, 44, 51, 52, 54, 64,
    68, 83, 84, 86, 93

seasonal · 11, 31, 32, 35, 44, 47, 52, 84, 86
segmentation · 33, 52, 93
selling · 5, 20, 41, 49, 50, 52, 71, 73, 78, 84, 88, 89
service · 20, 24, 27, 31, 33, 36, 43, 56, 66, 71, 72, 83, 85, 86, 87, 88, 90, 91, 92
Service · 74
service providers · 85
Sew in labels · 81
shopping experience · 20, 33, 35, 72, 74
shopping mall · 5, 72
shrinkage · 70, 88, 91
size · 28, 31, 35, 41, 42, 45, 46, 48, 49, 54, 55, 62, 64, 72, 74, 75, 76, 78, 81, 82, 84, 85, 86, 87, 88
Social and environmental responsibilities · 68
social media · 36, 44, 72, 92
Social responsibility · 92
sourcing specialist · 67
space · 31, 36, 48, 50, 73, 84, 85, 86, 87, 88, 89, 90, 91
special offers · 92
staffing · 28, 56, 71, 73, 74
standstill · 6
stock · 11, 31, 32, 38, 41, 46, 47, 49, 50, 51, 52, 61, 72, 73, 79, 80, 82, 83, 84, 85, 86, 87, 88, 89, 90, 91, 93
Stock Annual Turn · 20
Stock Forward Cover · 20
stock levels · 31, 38, 86, 87, 89, 93
stock turnover · 31
stocks · 30, 32, 47, 49, 51, 53, 84, 86, 88
storage · 55, 80, 83, 84, 85, 86, 87, 90, 91
store profiles · 32
stores · 5, 11, 20, 21, 24, 31, 32, 33, 35, 37, 38, 45, 48, 49, 51, 52, 71, 72, 73, 74, 79, 83, 84, 85, 86, 87, 88, 90, 94
strategic plan · 5, 6, 7, 18, 19
strategy · 6, 23, 24, 26, 27, 28, 30, 32, 33, 36, 38, 41, 42, 43, 50, 52, 56, 66, 67, 71, 74, 75, 77, 80, 83, 92, 93
strengths · 6, 68
Style briefing · 62
styles · 30, 32, 35, 42, 43, 44, 47, 48, 49, 52, 55, 74, 85
styling · 11, 29, 31, 37, 38, 43, 45, 52, 53, 55, 78
sub group · 28
sub groups · 28
Supplier introduction · 60
Supplier manuals · 61, 75
supplier performance · 27, 32
suppliers · 6, 24, 30, 32, 33, 41, 47, 53, 54, 55, 56, 57, 61, 62, 63, 66, 67, 68, 69, 74, 75, 76, 77, 79, 83, 85, 86, 87, 89, 93, 94
supply chain · 54, 55, 59, 61, 77, 83, 84, 85, 89, 91

T

target customer · 36, 41
target market · 25, 33, 55
tariffs · 83
teamwork · 31
technical · 6, 24, 29, 30, 31, 48, 53, 60, 63, 64, 66, 67, 68
technologists · 24, 32, 38, 52, 67, 69
technology · 24, 35, 54, 62, 67, 68, 69, 71, 78
Technology · 69, 74
themes · 31, 44, 47, 74, 84
thermal · 32, 67, 84
threads · 62, 67
threats · 6, 56, 66
Ticketing · 61
till · 29, 35, 72, 73, 92
trade shows · 24, 29
trading house · 54
trading houses · 54
training · 60
trend · 19, 26, 29, 31, 34, 35, 36, 42, 44, 52, 55, 71, 73, 79, 84
turnover · 28
types · 24, 28, 30, 43, 47, 49, 66, 67, 70, 71, 72, 75, 78, 89, 92

V

value added processing · 90
variety · 31, 42, 44

W

warehouse · 47, 55, 63, 80, 83, 84, 85, 86, 87, 88, 90
washability · 67
weaknesses · 6, 68
websites · 36, 62, 71, 72
weight · 61, 80
welfare · 92
width · 41, 78
working relationship · 67
workplace · 92
woven · 67
Woven · 78

Y

Yarns · 71

Referrals and acknowledgements

Bob Phibbs: (2010) *The Retail Doctor's guide to growing your business*, John Wiley & Sons, New Jersey

Business Plan Expert: (2014) *Fashion Business Plan Template,* Liraz Publishing

Meir Liraz: (2013) *Guide to Effective Retail Merchandise Management – a step by step guide to Merchandising in a Retail Store,* Liraz Publishing

Doug Stephens: (2013) *The Retail Revival: Reimagining business for the new age of consumerism,* John Wiley & Sons, Canada

Michelle Sackson: (2014) *The Ultimate Guide to Starting a Clothing Line,* K&K Publishing

Tim Jackson, David Shaw: (2001) *Mastering fashion buying & merchandising management,* Palgrave Macmillan

Rosemary Varley: (2014) *Retail Product Management Buying and merchandising,* Routledge

Judi Bevan: (2001) *The rise and fall of Marks & Spencer,* Profile Books Ltd

www.ingramcontent.com/pod-product-compliance
Lightning Source LLC
Chambersburg PA
CBHW051330170526
45166CB00002B/751